OCHA POLICY AND STUDIES SERIES

SAVING LIVES
TODAY
AND TOMORROW

MANAGING THE RISK OF HUMANITARIAN CRISES

ACKNOWLEDGMENTS

Research for this report was undertaken jointly by the UN Office for the Coordination of Humanitarian Affairs (OCHA) and DARA.

Managing Editor: Andrew Thow
Research and drafting team: Fernando Espada, Marybeth Redheffer, Daniela Ruegenberg, Andrea Noyes, Rodolpho Valente, Nathalie Guillaume
Editor: Mark Turner
Copy Editor: Nina Doyle
Design and layout: wearebold.es, Christina Samson

This report benefited from the feedback of our advisory group members: Dulce Chilundo, Ailsa Holloway, Randolph Kent, Pamela Komujuni, Toby Lanzer, Emanuel Tachie Obeng, Eva von Oelreich, Marianna Olinger, Kevin Savage, Hansjoerg Strohmeyer and Misikir Tilahun. Special thanks are due to the Chair of the advisory group, Sir John Holmes, for his commitment and guidance.

OCHA and DARA thank the hundreds of people who kindly shared their views and experience for this report, including OCHA and DARA staff for their valuable support, comments and suggestions. Thanks especially to OCHA staff in case-study countries (Burkina Faso, Indonesia, Kyrgyzstan and Tajikistan) and in regional offices, as their support, comments and suggestions were instrumental in the success of field research.

Thanks also to the Southern Africa Regional Inter-Agency Standing Committee, Ignacio Leon (Head of the OCHA Regional Office for Southern Africa) and Dr. Ailsa Holloway (Stellenbosch University) for their permission to integrate information and findings from Humanitarian Trends in Southern Africa: Challenges and Opportunities into this study.

Finally, we thank those experts who devoted their time to reviewing and discussing the study, including: Sandra Aviles, Rob Bailey, Rudi Coninx, Steve Darvill, François Grünewald, Nick Harvey, John Harding, Debbie Hillier, Yves Horent, Daniel Kull, Robert Piper and Rachel Scott.

Photo credits: Page 16 – OCHA / Zarina Nurmukhambetova, Page 32 – OCHA / David Ohana, Page 46 – FAO, Page 72 – OCHA.

This report was made possible by funding from Australia and Germany.

Produced by: OCHA Policy Analysis and Innovation Section, Policy Development and Studies Branch
Kirsten Gelsdorf, Chief, Policy Analysis and Innovation Section
Hansjoerg Strohmeyer, Chief, Policy Development and Studies Branch
For more information, please contact:
E-mail: ochapolicy@un.org
Tel: +1 917 367 4263

TABLE OF CONTENTS

MESSAGES FROM THE ADVISORY GROUP

The sad fact is that not only are humanitarian needs rising, as the rising world population faces increased risks from climate change, environmental degradation and the consequences of conflict, but anyone in the business also knows we need to do much more to reduce the impact of disasters before they happen, and to build local capacity. This report is another wake-up call to all concerned—humanitarian and development agencies, donors and affected Governments alike—to take our collective heads out of the sand, and apply more of our minds and our resources in these directions. There should be no more excuses.

John Holmes, former UN Emergency Relief Coordinator, Chair of the International Rescue Committee – UK, and author of "The Politics of Humanity" (Head of Zeus, 2013)

A timely, valid and indispensable piece of research, reminding us that response alone is unsustainable, and that collective early action saves not only lives, but increases development opportunities. We can heed the recommendations today, or wait for hazards to unceasingly challenge us, and for tomorrow's generation to judge us as a generation that could have done more but chose to do less.

Pamela Komujuni, Senior Disaster Management Officer, Office of the Prime Minister, Uganda

Although it is impossible to avert all disasters, measures can and must be taken to alleviate suffering before it happens. This study makes the case for a paradigm shift in the way we approach responses to humanitarian crises. While response is still critical, much has to be done to boost crisis prevention. And the task does not solely rest with humanitarian organizations. This is a study that should remain on the desk of all concerned with saving lives.

Misikir Tilahun, Head of Programmes, Africa Humanitarian Action

International disaster response cannot keep pace with burgeoning global challenges. Preventing catastrophes is possible, but this requires a new way of thinking and acting. Development and humanitarian actors, from local to global, need to reorient the way they operate to systematically analyse and manage risk. This study provides a compelling call for change. It also provides timely recommendations as the world looks towards the post-2015 framework for development and disaster risk reduction, alongside the 2016 World Humanitarian Summit.

Kevin Savage, Humanitarian Research Coordinator, World Vision International

Around the world, we are seeing the increasing impacts of shocks on local communities, from natural hazards to food-price rises and conflict. We are also seeing the profound benefits of supporting these communities to reduce and manage risks themselves, for example through community early warning and preparedness. Affected people don't see the institutional divides between humanitarian and development aid. They only know whether the support they get is relevant and useful and helps them to be independent. This report can help us make sure it is.

Eva von Oelreich, President, Swedish Red Cross

Disasters are not aberrant phenomena, but rather reflections of the ways people live their normal lives, and the ways societies prioritize and allocate resources. This study has more than sustained this point with practical insights and strategic perspectives.

Randolph Kent, Humanitarian Futures Programme, King's College London

As humanitarians it is vital to engage in political processes that shape the focus of governments, as well as the development agenda and the engagement of the private sector, if we are to move forward on the agenda of prevention and not only address symptoms or focus on humanitarian response.

Toby Lanzer, United Nations Resident Coordinator and Humanitarian Coordinator in South Sudan

Prevention is one of the most important strategies in saving lives. For that reason, Governments should invest to pursue this objective. This is why the motto for disaster management in Mozambique is, "It's better to prevent it than to fix it."

Dulce Fernanda M. Cabral Chilundo, General Director, National Institute for Information Technology and Communication, Ministry of Science and Technology, Mozambique

Implementing a risk-management approach to humanitarian crises requires significant changes: better collaboration between humanitarian and development communities; better sharing of risk analysis; integrated planning and programming; joined-up resource mobilization over five- to 10-year time frames. Risk management requires sustained focus and investment and is a marathon, not a sprint.

Hansjoerg Strohmeyer, Chief, Policy Development and Studies Branch, OCHA

This report brings together compelling evidence that humanitarian crises are not unexpected events, but the result of processes that develop throughout time and can have their impacts dramatically decreased, if not fully prevented. To put risk at the core of the aid is to embrace the knowledge and experience gained over several decades of practice.

Marianna Olinger, PhD in Urban and Regional Planning, Brazil

EXECUTIVE SUMMARY

The number of people affected by humanitarian crises has almost doubled over the past decade and is expected to keep rising. In early 2014, international aid organizations aimed to assist 52 million people in crisis, and millions more people sought help from their communities, local organizations and Governments. The cost of international humanitarian aid has more than trebled in the last 10 years, and responders are being asked to do more, at a greater cost, than ever before.

Global challenges—such as climate change, population growth, food- and energy-price volatility, water scarcity and environmental degradation—are increasing risks for vulnerable people. They are eroding people's ability to cope with shocks, making crises more protracted and recurrent, and undermining sustainable development. These trends have become as likely to cause humanitarian crises as disasters and conflicts.

A shift towards a more anticipatory and preventative approach to humanitarian crises is needed. Most crises can be predicted and, while they cannot always be prevented, the suffering they cause can often be greatly reduced. But humanitarian aid today is overwhelmingly focused on responding after crises occur. Governments and their partners have failed substantially to reduce risks to the world's most vulnerable people. It is time for a fundamental change in approach.

Crisis-risk management needs to be embedded in the humanitarian aid system. This includes systematically identifying risks, reducing their impact and coping with the residual effects. Currently, action following the warning signs of crises is often late or insufficient, and funding is too focused on response. Long-term aid is not helping the most vulnerable people to build resilience. Every humanitarian crisis is different, but a risk-management approach can and should be applied universally. It should go hand in hand with responding to need.

Humanitarian organizations cannot do this alone. Preventing and mitigating crises requires the commitment of Governments, development organizations and many others. When Governments take the lead, they save more lives, avert economic losses and foster sustainable development. Government leadership encourages humanitarian and development organizations to work more effectively together and multiplies their impact.

Humanitarian and development organizations need to transcend the institutional divide that separates them. This divide inhibits programmes that can help people manage risk, such as preparedness and livelihoods support. They need to agree common risk-management and resilience objectives, and to achieve them through joint analysis, planning, programming and funding.

National and local capacity is critical to successful risk management. Humanitarian organizations already work with Governments to manage crisis risk, but their role is rarely systematic and their services are difficult to access outside crises, which is when everyone is focused on response. Governments and humanitarian organizations need to build a better-defined, less-politicized and longer-term relationship.

There needs to be better analysis of the risks that lead to crises and more effective systems to respond when risks are identified. This can include more sophisticated risk models and triggers, as well as forums to share analysis and address risks. Joint analysis and planning between humanitarian and development organizations are critical. The timing of humanitarian and development planning also needs to be aligned.

There is insufficient assistance for people to prevent and mitigate crises and increase resilience. The majority of humanitarian aid comprises material assistance (food, water, shelter, health care), even when crisis has become the norm. Good programming helps people address risk in a holistic way, addressing current and future challenges. Social-protection mechanisms, such as cash-transfer programming, need to be dramatically scaled up.

Not enough funding goes to risk-management activities. Prevention-and-preparedness funding comprised less than 0.5 per cent of all international aid over the past 20 years, and most came from humanitarian budgets. Assistance to prevent crises rarely goes to the people and countries most at risk. New funding mechanisms are not required, but funding based on objective and shared assessment of crisis risk is essential. Insurance and other risk-transfer tools offer opportunities to better manage crisis risk.

There is insufficient leadership in humanitarian organizations to improve risk management. Aid agencies need to honestly examine their organizational structures , incentives, processes and culture. Senior leaders need to champion and be accountable for managing crisis risk, and concerted advocacy is needed to bring it to the attention of decision makers. The 2016 World Humanitarian Summit and post-2015 development agenda offer excellent opportunities to do this.

This report presents a humanitarian perspective on a challenge that goes far beyond the humanitarian sector. The shift from cure to prevention is ultimately a political challenge that requires the will and efforts of Governments, development organizations, civil society, private companies and many others. This report is intended to start a global dialogue, to change the way we do business. We cannot afford not to do so.

Summary of recommendations

Make preventing future humanitarian crises a priority

Prioritize crisis-risk management. Address risk through all functions; provide livelihood options, basic services and social protection for the vulnerable; and set up systems for crisis anticipation, preparedness and response.

Increase and formalize role in managing crisis risk, work more closely with Governments to build capacity. Provide aid that meets immediate needs and addresses future risk.

Create new partnerships and incentives

Support and develop joint initiatives that contribute to crisis anticipation, prevention, mitigation and recovery and commit resources to those initiatives. Strengthen links between humanitarian and development teams through joint planning cells.

Work differently and systematically address risk

Base planning on a common analysis of risk and align planning cycles where possible. Support tools and processes to jointly analyse crisis risk, such as the InfoRM initiative.

Increase the capacity of the RC/HC for risk analysis and strategic planning, for example through an expert roster system.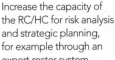

Dedicate resources today to save lives tomorrow

Base crisis prevention and mitigation funding decisions on risk analysis. Ensure sufficient funds flow through existing mechanisms to support the people and countries at highest risk of crises.

Ensure development aid targets people and countries most at risk from crises. Integrate crisis risk into national development plans, bilateral agreements. Specifically include it in the post-2015 development agenda.

Launch a global advocacy campaign on preventing humanitarian crises, focused on the post-2015 development agenda and World Humanitarian Summit. Use high-level 'global champions'.

Establish a national coordination forum to jointly analyse and address risks, monitor and share early warning information, and develop triggers for action.

Appoint senior leaders with responsibility for crisis-risk management, as well as Regional HCs to help align risk-management work of Governments, international organizations and donors.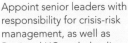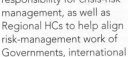

Increase the length of planning cycle to three years in protracted crises. Increase use of programmatic approaches—including preparedness, livelihood support and cash-transfer programming—to help communities manage the risk of crises.

Ensure existing funding mechanisms are reviewed and adjusted to maximize their contribution to managing crisis risk. Dedicate a higher proportion of core funding to activities that help manage crisis risk.

Work with the private sector and other relevant partners to increase the use of risk-transfer mechanisms, such as risk mutualization and micro-insurance.

 Host governments   Donor governments   Humanitarian organizations   Development organizations

Note: This is an abridged version of the report's recommendations. See Chapter 4 for the complete version.

INTRODUCTION

The international aid system at a crossroads

The instinct to help is as old as humanity. Support to a friend in need, aid to a neighbour in crisis, and acts of altruism and solidarity are all essential to who we are.

However, something new has emerged over recent decades. We have translated this instinct into an international enterprise, creating a global humanitarian system to assist people across the world. Over time, this system has become larger, more complex and more expensive. Today, it employs thousands of people, costs billions of dollars and has helped save millions of lives.

But despite these efforts, the number of people in crisis is growing. Around the planet, we see the poorest and most vulnerable people struggling with a growing number of shocks and stresses, affecting their ability to survive and care for their families. As the scale of this challenge grows, we are increasingly questioning the humanitarian system's capacity to deliver.

Humanitarian organizations face a choice: Should they continue to respond to the growing number of people affected by crises, with the commensurate increase in resources and efficiency gains that this will require? Or is a more fundamental shift required, towards a model which—working with Governments and the development sector—not only fine tunes and improves the response to humanitarian crises, but learns to anticipate them, to act before they become catastrophes and to prevent their recurrence?

An increasing number of experts and practitioners are concluding that the second option is not only preferable, but essential. This report aims to explain why, and how to make that shift a reality.

52 million

Number of people to receive international humanitarian aid in 2014. If all these people lived in one country, it would be the 25th most populous in the world.[1]

An interplay of shocks

Figure 1

Nepalese farmer Manbahadur Tamang (Photo: IRIN)

Take the story of Manbahadur Tamang, a subsistence farmer in Kolpata village, 150 km from the Nepali capital, Kathmandu. In December 2012, heavy rains destroyed his family's entire crop. The family had no safety net and did not have enough cash to buy food, which had doubled in price over the previous five years. They were forced to seek work as casual labourers, and Tamang's teenage sons had to drop out of school.

It is a classic tale of modern crisis. Multiple stresses—including worsening weather, political uncertainty and tightening economic conditions—combined to create a chronically challenging situation, in which no single response was sufficient.

"My main concern is that food prices will go up again. It's such a headache because the price of the fuel is spiraling, which directly impacts the price of food, oil and transport," Tamang explained. He was also worried about the political situation in his country, which is still recovering from a decade-long civil war. "[It] remains uncertain… We can only hope that things get better."[23]

Tamang is not alone. Chronic poverty and vulnerability mean that for millions of people worldwide, even a small shock, such as lower-than-normal rainfall or illness of a family member, can push them into a situation of crisis. In Tamang's case, better management of flood risks and a safety net could have made a significant difference.

More people affected, more often and for longer

The number of people targeted by international humanitarian assistance has almost doubled over the last decade. Inter-agency appeals typically aim to assist 50 to 70 million people each year, compared with 30 to 40 million 10 years ago (figure 2).[4] Funding requirements have more than trebled to over US$10 billion per year.

The length of intervention has also expanded. Traditionally, humanitarian assistance was seen as a stop-gap; a short-term show of international support to help people weather a shock and get back on their feet. Today, protracted and recurrent crises have become the norm. Of the 22 countries that had an inter-agency appeal in 2012, 21 had at least one other crisis in the previous 10 years (figure 3). Eight countries had eight or more crises.[5] Humanitarian aid agencies are finding themselves on the ground for years on end.

Economic development has delivered enormous gains for billions of people around the world, but more than 1.2 billion people still live on less than $1.25 a day.[6] More than 840 million people are chronically undernourished.[7] Poverty is becoming more concentrated in fragile states, where 50 per cent of the world's extreme poor will live by 2014.[8]

Humanitarian needs and funding requirements

Figure 2

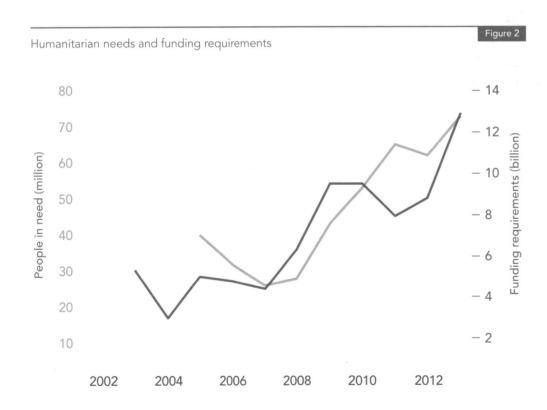

The convergence of new global trends is increasing the risk of major crises, their scope and their complexity. These include climate change, population growth, unplanned urbanization, mass migration, and food and water insecurity. For example, the food-price crisis of 2007/8 demonstrated how commodity-price shocks can rapidly increase humanitarian needs across many countries simultaneously.

A global deficit has emerged in the operational and financial capacity of Governments and humanitarian organizations to respond.

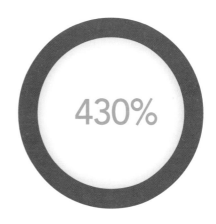

430%

Increase in total global funding requirements of annual inter-agency humanitarian appeals between 2004 and 2013[9]

Figure 3

Inter-agency appeals by year for countries with an appeal in 2012

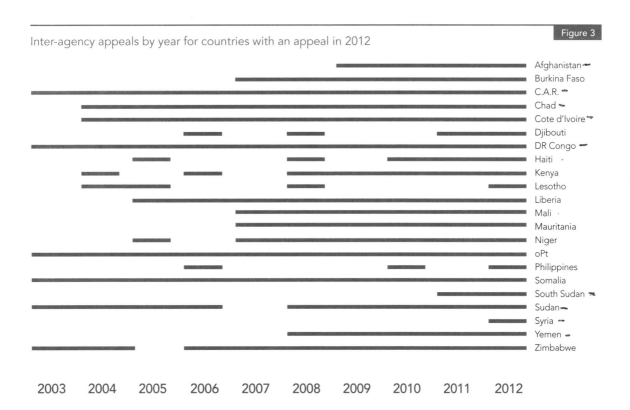

Afghanistan
Burkina Faso
C.A.R.
Chad
Cote d'Ivoire
Djibouti
DR Congo
Haiti
Kenya
Lesotho
Liberia
Mali
Mauritania
Niger
oPt
Philippines
Somalia
South Sudan
Sudan
Syria
Yemen
Zimbabwe

2003   2004   2005   2006   2007   2008   2009   2010   2011   2012

From response to anticipation

The debate between business-as-usual or shifting to a model focused on anticipation and prevention is not new, but it is taking on increasing urgency.

One example is the Sahel region of Africa, which has been called "ground zero"

for climate change.[10] Recurrent droughts have affected the Sahel since the 1970s, each followed by an increase in people's vulnerability. In 2005, 7 million Sahelians struggled to feed themselves. In 2010, that number rose to 10 million people, and in 2012 it grew to more than 18 million. Development indicators have slowly improved, but they remain among the worst of any region worldwide (figure 4).

Food crises and development indicators in the Sahel (source: OCHA, World Bank)

Figure 4

| 7 million | | 10 million | 18 million | 11 million |

Food insecure

2005   2006   2007   2008   2009   2010   2011   2012   2013

Life expectancy
48 in 2000
53 in 2012

Under 5 mortality rate
167 in 2000
127 in 2012

Access to water
53% in 2000
61% in 2012

Access to sanitation
31% in 2000
30% in 2012

Neither decades-long development programmes nor food-aid interventions could address the root causes of these crises. Humanitarian aid remained focused on responding to immediate needs, while economic-development programmes could not break the cycle of poverty and vulnerability.

Governments and aid organizations have agreed that they must take a longer-term approach, aligning humanitarian and development work to help people better manage risks and build their resilience to future shocks.

Other regions have switched to a more prevention-focused approach. After the cyclone in Odisha caused 10,000 deaths on the eastern coast of India in 1999, the Government built shelters, strengthened embankments, planned evacuation routes and conducted drills. In October 2013, as Cyclone Phailin headed for the coast, nearly 1 million people were evacuated. But while similar in scale to the 1999 storm, it caused only 38 deaths.

"In 1992, all our houses were completely destroyed. This time the houses weren't all destroyed, even though the level of floodwater was higher, because we were prepared. This year, we were more careful. We kept all our assets and carried them to the emergency shelter, and we made embankments around the houses to stop the water from coming."

Syeda, South Punjab, Pakistan, 2010[11]

From managing crisis to managing risk

When crisis strikes, local communities are the first to help people in need, and national Governments are primarily responsible for overseeing the response. If the crisis overwhelms local and national capacity, or in situations of conflict, international humanitarian organizations offer support.

Historically, this assistance has focused on responding to emergencies as and when they occur. In 2011, less than 5 per cent of all humanitarian aid was used for prevention and preparedness,[12] and those activities comprised less than 0.5 per cent of the $3 trillion spent in international aid between 1991 and 2010.[13]

But in most cases, humanitarian crises are predictable Their worst effects can be mitigated, or even prevented, leaving hope for a sustainable recovery in which people rebuild their lives and become more resilient to future crises.

In practice, many humanitarian organizations already go beyond life-saving interventions, helping communities and Governments prepare for emergencies, supporting people's livelihoods and helping them recover from disasters. But most of these activities have taken place in a largely non-systematic way.

To shift focus requires more than fine-tuning the way humanitarian organizations currently respond. It calls for a profound change in the way humanitarian organizations understand their role, the places where they work and their links with other aid actors and Governments.

More than 500 experts interviewed for this report agreed that humanitarian assistance needs to contribute more to anticipation and prevention, as well as recovery from crises.

There was less agreement, however, on the extent of the change required and how to implement it. Some were concerned that humanitarian organizations are taking on more responsibilities than they can cope with, and that their mission is growing too large.

Managing crisis risk is not something humanitarian organizations can, or should, do alone. It requires wider changes to the way Governments, development organizations and others work to support vulnerable people.

This report argues that all aid actors should recognize their shared responsibility to people at risk of crisis, prioritize their efforts according to the risks they face and join forces to help them manage the risks. It looks at how this work could be enhanced within a broader network of activities by international organizations, donors and Government authorities.

The report proposes that humanitarian and development efforts must urgently be aligned through joint analysis, planning and programming, funding, leadership and advocacy. Humanitarian and development organizations must transcend the artificial divide between them and address crisis risk according to their comparative advantages.

This is not the first time this appeal has been made. But the debate has been reinvigorated by recent crises, such as the global food-price hikes of 2007/8; huge floods in Pakistan in 2010 and 2011; conflict, earthquakes and typhoons in the Philippines; and recurring drought in the Horn of Africa and the Sahel.

"People have always dealt with disasters like firefighters, as if the risks were completely unavoidable. After the emergency, with the job done, the brave firemen go back to the station, applause ringing in their ears, to wait in 'stand-by' mode for the next alert."

Youcef Ait-Chellouche, IFRC[14]

The timing is right. The world is gearing up to create a new global development framework after 2015, which is likely to require a more integrated approach to poverty reduction and sustainable development. A new agreement will replace the Hyogo Framework for Action on Disaster Risk Reduction in 2015.[15] And a World Humanitarian Summit is scheduled for 2016, in which managing crisis risk is likely to top the agenda.

Although many practical, incremental improvements can and should be made now, the report suggests that a transformation is required; a shift in the way we think about emergencies—from human tragedies that we respond to in the present, to ones we prevent in the future.

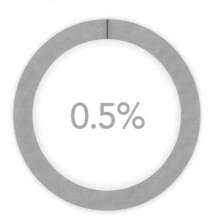

0.5%

Proportion of all international aid used for prevention and preparedness between 1991 and 2010[16]

5%

Proportion of humanitarian aid used for prevention and preparedness in 2011[17]

Study methods and report structure

Research for this study was undertaken by OCHA and DARA, an independent research organization. It employed a mixed-methods approach, including literature review, interviews with more than 100 people from Governments, aid agencies and civil-society groups, an online survey with more than 500 responses, and field research in Burkina Faso, Central Asia and Indonesia.

The study also benefited from research on Southern Africa carried out by Stellenbosch University.[18] An advisory group comprising humanitarian aid workers, Government representatives and experts helped guide the study.

The report is divided into four chapters:

Chapter 1 explores the challenges and risks facing people today and how they can lead to humanitarian crises.

Chapter 2 looks at how humanitarian assistance is contributing to managing crisis risk and the barriers to effective risk management.

Chapter 3 discusses how the humanitarian sector can improve its contribution to managing the risk of crises based on existing best practices and opportunities for improvement.

Chapter 4 presents conclusions and recommendations based on extensive field and desk research and direct feedback from hundreds of experts.

Multiple shocks

A family from the Khatlon area of central Tajikistan stands in front of their house, which has been damaged by flash floods and mud-flows. Half of the population in the area is vulnerable to food insecurity because of recurrent disasters and high food prices. Soil erosion in the region has increased the risk of flooding.

CHAPTER 1
Risks and Consequences

Chapter Takeaways

▶ The number of people who need humanitarian assistance and the cost of helping them is increasing. Global trends—such as climate change, population growth, rapid and unplanned urbanization, food and water [insecurity,] poverty, inequality and [mass migration]—are increasing the risk of humanitarian crises. *what kind of?*

▶ Humanitarian experts consider these new drivers of crisis just as important as disasters and conflict. While they think that humanitarian organizations need to adapt to the changing risk landscape, they are not currently confident in their ability to do so.

▶ Humanitarian crises are still treated as discrete events, with insufficient analysis or treatment of their underlying causes and too little in the way of comprehensive actions by Governments and development and humanitarian organizations to prevent and manage them.

"Responding to the dramatic increase in extreme weather events and mega-disasters is one of the great challenges of our present age. Climate change, rapid urbanization and population growth in hazard-prone cities and coastal areas make action all the more urgent."

United Nations Secretary-General
Ban Ki-moon[19]

This chapter outlines some basic concepts related to risk. It explores the challenges facing people vulnerable to crisis in today's world, how those risks can converge to cause humanitarian crises, and the perspectives of humanitarian practitioners on risks. It also describes the risk landscape in case studies for [Burkina Faso, Central Asia, Indonesia and Southern Africa.] *where?*

Global challenges and the changing risk landscape

Worldwide, there is an increase in the number of people who need humanitarian assistance and the cost of helping them.[20]

The number of armed conflicts has declined over the past 20 years, but more people are being uprooted by violence. Forty-five million people were displaced at the end of 2012–the most since 1994.[21]

Natural disasters are increasing. Over the last 10 years there was an average of 320 recorded disasters a year, compared with 290 in the previous 10 years.[22] Mortality risk related to floods, winds and droughts is decreasing thanks to investment in early warning systems, better preparedness and economic development. But the number of people exposed to severe weather is increasing. Between 1970 and 2010, the world's population increased by 87 per cent, but the population exposed to flooding increased by 114 per cent. Mortality risk relating to earthquakes and tsunamis is also growing due to a rise in people living in areas at risk.[23]

The role of natural hazards, exposure and vulnerability in disaster risk

Figure 5

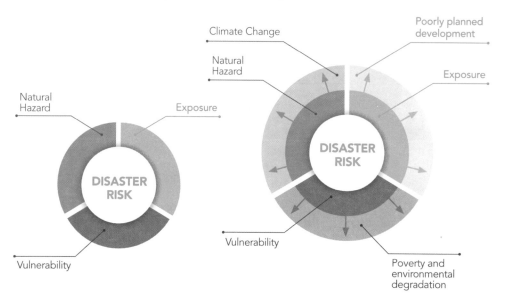

Disaster risk is determined by the occurrence of a natural hazard (e.g. a cyclone), which may impact exposed populations and assets (e.g. houses located in the cyclone path). Vulnerability is the characteristic of the population or asset making it particularly susceptible to damaging effects (e.g. fragility of housing construction). Poorly planned development, poverty, environmental degradation and climate change can increase the magnitude of this interaction, leading to larger disasters. From World Bank (2013).[24]

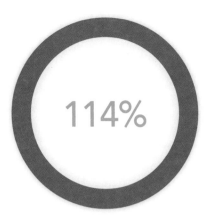

114%

Global increase in the number of people exposed to flooding between 1970 and 2010. The world's population increased by 87% in the same period.[25]

Underlying drivers, such as poverty, badly planned and managed urban and regional development, and ecosystem decline, are increasing the risk of disaster from these events (figure 5). For example, the earthquake that killed more than 200,000 people in Haiti in 2010 was devastating not just because of its strength (a much stronger earthquake in Chile the same year killed less than 500 people), but because of a failure to enforce minimal building standards. Moreover, the earthquake hit people still recovering from previous crises, including hurricanes, political violence and the 2007/8 food-price crisis, and who were living in a critically degraded environment.[26]

Figure 6

Resilience and vulnerability compared

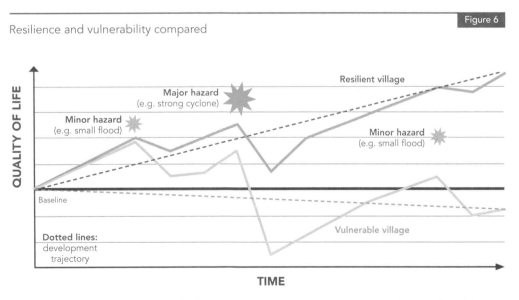

The chart shows how the quality of life changes over time in two communities—one that is resilient (blue) and one that is vulnerable (orange). Over the observed time frame, both villages are affected three times by a hazard. Three observations are made for the resilient village: First, the immediate hazard impact is smaller; second, the recovery is faster; and third, the overall development trajectory is more positive. The implication of these observations is that reinforcing resilience is important not just in the context of crisis-risk management, but also of development. From Banyaneer (2013).[27]

From global risk to local crisis

Disasters and conflict have been understood as the main drivers of humanitarian need, but a number of global trends are changing the humanitarian risk landscape (figure 8). Climate change, population growth, rapid and unplanned urbanization, food and water insecurity, poverty, inequality and mass migration all contribute to an increased risk of humanitarian crises.

Climate change is contributing to weather and climate extremes and is expected to do so more over time. For example, the maximum wind speed of tropical cyclones is likely to increase. Typhoon Haiyan, which destroyed parts of the Philippines in November 2013, was the most powerful

Figure 7

Global food-price index and the occurrence of food riots (number of casualties in brackets). Food riots in Yemen are marked orange. From Gros et al (2012).

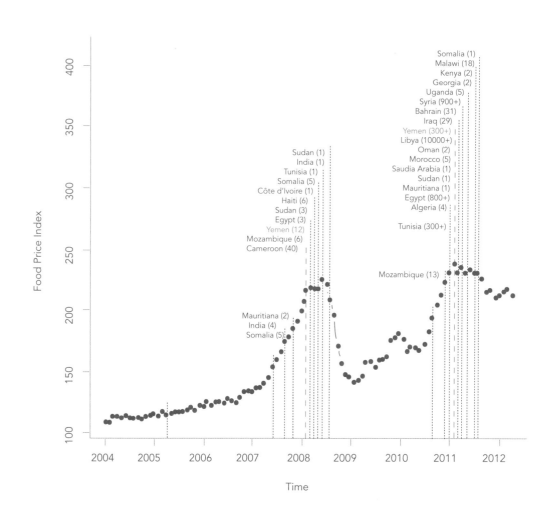

typhoon ever recorded to hit land. UN Secretary-General Ban Ki-moon called it a "wake-up call."[28]

Climate change is also leading to more food insecurity in regions such as the Sahel and the Horn of Africa, threatening the livelihoods of millions.[29] These and other effects—such as sea-level rise—could lead to large-scale displacement, with serious adverse consequences for human security and economic and trade systems.[30]

High and volatile commodity prices may increase civil unrest. Food-price rises in 2007/8 led to protests in almost 50 countries (figure 7).[31] In Yemen, food riots triggered violence that spread to the endemically poor southern region,[32] and half the population now requires humanitarian assistance.[33] High food prices were also seen as a precipitating condition for the so-called Arab spring.[34]

Environmental degradation, whether driven by climate change or other human activities, can increase crisis risk. Deforestation and desertification affect rainfall patterns, can lead to landslides and worsen the effects of flooding. Destruction of natural protection, such as mangroves, dunes and reefs, increases exposure to coastal hazards.[35] Environmental degradation can make conflict more likely, as in Darfur and the Sahel.[36] [37]

50

Number of countries that experienced food price protests in 2007-2008[38]

Population growth is likely to play a role in future humanitarian crises. The number of people living in countries that issued an inter-agency humanitarian appeal in 2013 is expected almost to double by 2050, suggesting caseloads will increase.[39] Countries where young adults comprise more than 40 per cent of the population are twice as likely to experience a new outbreak of civil conflict.[40] If economies do not keep pace with populations, youth unemployment and underemployment (especially among unmarried males) could trigger social instability.

Rapid and unplanned urbanization has been linked with an increased risk of civil conflict, as well as disaster risk. The urban population in countries that issued inter-agency humanitarian appeals in 2013 will increase by more than 250 per cent by 2050. Malaria, tuberculosis and HIV/AIDS are more likely to spread in urban centres with poor sanitation facilities and high population density.[41]

When combined, these factors have an even greater effect. For example, the combination of rapid urban growth, a youth increase and low per-capita availability of cropland and fresh water can increase a country's risk of civil conflict.[42] This was the case during ethnic clashes between Uzbeks and Kyrgyzs in Kyrgyzstan in 2010.

Climate Change

Climate change is likely to increase crisis risk significantly as a result of changes in weather and climate extremes, sea level rise and impacts on water availability, ecosystems, agriculture and human health. These could lead to large-scale displacement and have adverse consequences for human security and economic and trade systems. Impacts are expected to multiply. Extreme precipitation events over mid-latitude and tropical regions will very likely become more intense and more frequent by 2100, contributing to increased flooding.

Population growth

In 2013, the global population reached 7.2 billion. By 2050, it is expected to reach 9.6 billion. Most of the growth will occur in developing regions, which are projected to increase from 5.9 billion in 2013 to 8.2 billion in 2050. The proportion of global population living in current LDCs will increase to 27% by 2100. By 2050, the population of the countries that have a Consolidated Humanitarian Appeal (CAP) in 2013 will have doubled. Countries where young adults comprise more than 40 per cent of the population were two and a half times more likely to experience a new outbreak of civil conflict in the 1990s.

Food security

One in eight people in the world are estimated to be suffering from chronic hunger. Africa remains the region with the highest prevalence of undernourishment, with more than one in five people hungry. By 2050, global demand for food is expected to have increased by 70%. High and volatile food and commodity prices over recent years have exacerbated the food and nutrition insecurity of poor households.

Energy security

Global energy demand will rise by one-third between 2013 and 2035, with 90% of the increase coming from emerging economies. The availability and affordability of energy is a critical element of economic well-being. Recent energy price shocks have increased food insecurity and poverty in developing countries. Energy price shocks tend to have a stronger effect on poorer households.

Poverty and inequality

Persistence of extreme poverty or increases in inequality could result in increased instability and resulting humanitarian need when combined with other factors. As of 2010, 1.22 billion people still live on less than US$1.25 a day. Between 2005 and 2015, the proportion of people living in extreme poverty in Sub-Saharan Africa will decrease from 50.9% to 35.8% (388 million to 345 million). Africa's share of global poverty will more than double from 28 to 60% between 2005 and 2015. By 2014, the proportion of the world's poor living in fragile states will reach 50%.

Urbanization

The number of people living in urban areas will reach 6.3 billion by 2050. Urban areas will absorb all the population growth expected over the next four decades, while at the same time drawing in some of the rural population. Between 2010 and 2050, the urban population will increase by 200% in Africa, and 100% in Asia. By 2050, half of the people in LDCs will be living in urban areas.

Water security

Between 1990 and 2010, two billion people gained access to improved drinking water sources. However, 11% of the global population, or 783 million people, are still without access to drinking water. Global water withdrawals have tripled in the last 50 years, but the reliable supply of water has stayed relatively constant. By 2030 it is projected that 47% of world population will be living in areas of high water stress. In developing countries, about 80% of illnesses are linked to poor water and sanitation conditions.

Health

Non-communicable diseases are currently the leading cause of death across the world - with the exception of Sub-Saharan Africa. Four out of five deaths from non-communicable diseases occur in low and middle-income countries. Thirty-four percent of all deaths are caused by infectious disease, while deaths from war account for only 0.64 percent. Neglected tropical diseases affect one billion people, normally in the poorest communities, with consequences of permanent disability, extreme pain and death.

Sources: FAO[43], IEA[44], IPCC[45], UNDESA[46], UNESCO[47], UNWATER[48], OECD[49], Ravallion & Chen (2012)[50], Vafeidis et al (2011)[51], WHO/UNICEF[52], World Bank[53]

Figure 8

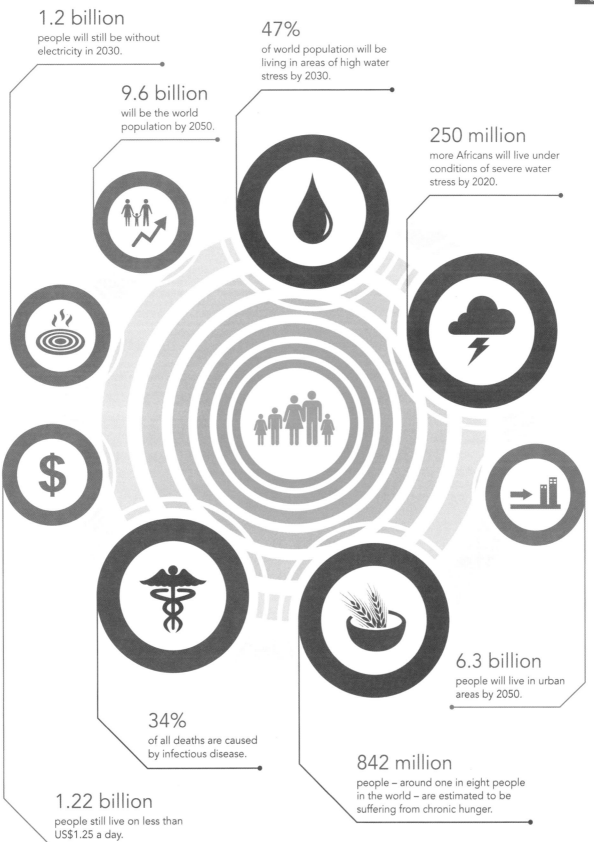

1.2 billion
people will still be without electricity in 2030.

9.6 billion
will be the world population by 2050.

47%
of world population will be living in areas of high water stress by 2030.

250 million
more Africans will live under conditions of severe water stress by 2020.

6.3 billion
people will live in urban areas by 2050.

842 million
people – around one in eight people in the world – are estimated to be suffering from chronic hunger.

34%
of all deaths are caused by infectious disease.

1.22 billion
people still live on less than US$1.25 a day.

Key concepts

A **humanitarian crisis** is an event or series of events that represents a critical threat to the health, safety, security or well-being of a community or other large group of people, usually over a wide area.[54]

Risk is the combination of the probability of an event and its negative consequences.[55] It is the result of hazardous events interacting with vulnerable social conditions.[56]

Hazards are potential threats to human life and livelihoods. They include natural hazards and man-made hazards such as conflicts, technological and industrial accidents, as well as other shocks, such as price spikes.

Exposure refers to the presence of people, livelihoods, environmental services, resources and infrastructure, or economic, social or cultural assets in places that could be adversely affected.[57]

"We must stop calling events like these [Typhoon Haiyan/ Yolanda] natural disasters. Disasters are never natural. They are the intersection of factors other than physical. They are the accumulation of the constant breach of economic, social and environmental thresholds."

Yeb Sano, Philippines climate negotiator[58]

Vulnerability refers to the capacity of an individual or group to anticipate, cope with, resist and recover from the impact of a natural or man-made hazard. Vulnerability is a result of many pre-existing physical, social, economic and environmental factors.[59]

Resilience refers to the ability of a community or society exposed to hazards to resist, absorb, accommodate and recover from the effects of a hazard in a timely and efficient manner (figure 6).[60]

Risk management is the process of confronting risks, preparing for them and coping with their effects. Its goals are twofold: a) resilience—the ability of people, societies and countries to recover from negative shocks; and b) prosperity—derived from successfully managing positive shocks that create opportunities for development.[61] This study is about managing contextual risks—those that are external to humanitarian organizations. It does not cover the management of programmatic or internal risks, which relates to the operation of organizations (e.g. programme failure, misappropriation of aid, reputational damage).[62]

315
km/hour

Peak wind speed of Typhoon Haiyan, the most powerful storm ever recorded to strike land[63]

"Our season is changing. We don't know when there will be a bad year and when there will be a good year."

Selas Samson Biru, farmer in Northern Ethiopia[64]

Perspectives on risk

As part of this study, more than 500 experts from 90 countries took part in an online survey on risk, and how the humanitarian system could help anticipate and prevent crises. They considered climate change, poverty and inequality, disasters, food insecurity, economic instability, and violence and armed conflicts to be the factors most likely to increase vulnerability (figure 9).

This is in line with warnings from other sectors. For example, business leaders expressed similar concerns about water, energy, food and climate change in the World Economic Forum's annual survey of global risks.[65] Climate change, international financial instability and Islamic extremist groups top the concerns of Africans, according the Pew Global Attitudes survey.[66]

Figure 9

Most important risks from the perspective of humanitarian experts
How important do you think the following issues will be in increasing vulnerability in the future?

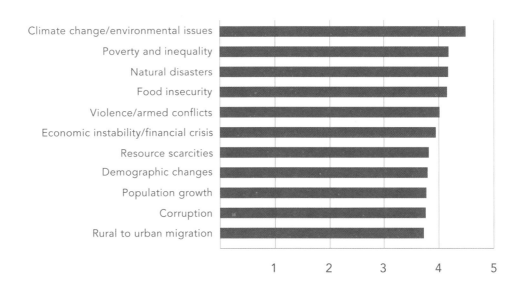

A multifaceted response to multidimensional crises

Humanitarian crises have always been complex, and humanitarian organizations have always adapted to changing risks and circumstances. But the challenges and trends described above will affect more people, and involve more factors, than humanitarian organizations have the capacity, expertise and mandate to manage alone. The way they respond to emergencies will need to change.

Traditionally, crises have been treated as discrete events, with insufficient analysis or treatment of their underlying causes and little in the way of comprehensive responses. But the risks people face are multidimensional and cannot be addressed in isolation. For example, responding to the 2007/8 food-price crisis required political, economic, agricultural and humanitarian interventions by Governments and development and humanitarian organizations.[67] No single actor can address the changing face of crises alone.

Tajikistan's three-way crisis: food, water and energy

In 2007/8, Tajikistan experienced its harshest winter in 30 years. It severely affected energy and water supplies, hindered access to hospitals, limited food production and restricted the distribution of essential commodities. As neighbouring countries were also affected, the energy supply to Tajikistan was limited and the price of alternative fuels increased, resulting in a severe energy shortage.[68]

People were already struggling to deal with rocketing food prices due to the previous summer's drought and the global food-price crisis. The extreme poverty rate, which had fallen by 2.5 times between 2003 and 2007, stagnated from 2007 to 2009, and in some provinces it increased. Approximately 60 per cent of affected Tajik households reduced their food consumption.[69]

This combination of shocks led to a humanitarian crisis affecting more than 2 million people. Shahnoza Abdulloeva is a 16-year-old student from Rudaki, a district surrounding the capital, Dushanbe. For her, the crisis meant limited access to water and a disruption in her school routine.

"We avoid going outside except when coming to school and collecting water. This is another problem we face this winter, since we have to collect water over long distances," she said. "Last week my mother allowed me to attend school, but my younger sister stayed at home because of the cold." In her school, attendance dropped between 50 and 60 per cent.

In the face of recurrent energy crises, some households started to stock up on supplies ahead of time, to better cope with severe winters. "We have no electricity at home or in school," said Shahnoza. "But our home is quite warm, as my parents stored coal and wood during the summer because we anticipated a cold winter."[70]

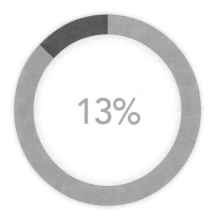

13%

Proportion of surveyed experts that think the humanitarian system is prepared for new risks

Can the humanitarian system adapt?

Is the humanitarian system well prepared to adapt and respond to these new challenges? According to a survey for this study, experts are not confident in the humanitarian system. Only 13 per cent of respondents consider that it is very or completely prepared (figure 10). Nevertheless, 91 per cent of respondents think that anticipation and prevention of crises are very or completely important for humanitarian organizations.

Figure 10

Is the humanitarian system prepared to anticipate and prevent humanitarian crises?

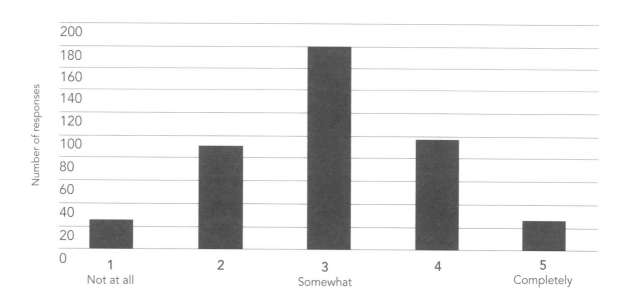

Humanitarian risk in Indonesia, Central Asia, Burkina Faso and South Africa

Three field-research missions (Indonesia, Burkina Faso and Central Asia–Kyrgyzstan and Tajikistan) were conducted for this report. Findings of another study, *Humanitarian Trends in Southern Africa: Challenges and Opportunities*[71] were also incorporated into its findings.

These countries and regions were selected not because they represent today's largest humanitarian crises, but because they shed light on the interplay of crisis risks. This section presents brief summaries of the risk landscape in each country or region. It is intended as background.

Further analysis, including of how local and international actors understand and manage risks in each country and region, as well as the findings of research carried out during the field missions is incorporated throughout this report.

Indonesia

Indonesia is one of the world's most disaster-prone countries in the world's most disaster-prone region. Since the Indian Ocean tsunami in 2004, which claimed over 150,000 lives, there have been several major emergencies in that country.

The Yogyakarta earthquake in 2006 killed more than 5,000 people and injured 15,000, "reducing hundreds of buildings to rubble, severing essential services and damaging roads and airport runways."[72] The West Java earthquake in 2009 damaged 65,000 houses, killing 72 people and displacing 88,000.[73] In 2009, several earthquakes in West Sumatra killed 1,000 people and injured another 2,000.[74][75] In 2010, a tsunami off the coast of Sumatra and the eruption of Mount Merapi in Java killed more than 600 people and displaced hundreds of thousands.[76]

The number of disaster-related deaths in Indonesia has declined, but an increasing number of people live in highly exposed areas, and the number of people affected by crisis is increasing.

Between 2000 and 2010, Indonesia's urban population grew from 85.2 million to 118.3 million, concentrated predominantly in coastal areas. This was accompanied by inappropriate urban planning and deficient building standards, exacerbating the potential damage caused by earthquakes, floods or landslides.

In January 2013, for example, seasonal rains flooded several districts in Jakarta, including the city centre and Government buildings, affecting 250,000 people and displacing 40,000. The deficiencies of the capital's infrastructure (drainage system, canals and water reservoirs) were accentuated by a weather event that was neither extraordinary nor unpredictable.

33 million

Growth of Indonesia's urban population between 2000 and 2010, mainly in coastal areas[77]

Central Asia
(Kyrgyzstan and Tajikistan)

Kyrgyzstan and Tajikistan are among the most vulnerable countries in Central Asia: landlocked, low income and highly dependent on the outside world for food and energy.

In Kyrgyzstan, almost 40 per cent of people are below the poverty line, and one third struggle to feed themselves. Kyrgyz frequently face earthquakes, floods, landslides and extreme winters, as well as political instability, ethnic tensions and a lack of investment in infrastructure or basic services.

In 2010, political demonstrations in the south evolved into extremely violent ethnic clashes in Osh and Jalal-Abad, killing almost 500 people and displacing more than 400,000 ethnic Uzbeks. Grievances included insufficient clean water, the decline of agricultural economy, a lack of clarity over grazing rights and poor access to education.

In Tajikistan, almost half the population lives on less than $1.50 a day and 17 per cent on less than $1 a day. Most people spend between 60 and 80 per cent of their income on food, and one third are food insecure. Remittances—mostly from workers in the Russian Federation—account for almost 50 per cent of GDP, and they are the main income source for almost 55 per cent of rural households.

Transparency International ranks Kyrgyzstan and Tajikistan among the most corrupt countries in the world. Nevertheless, during the 1990s and the 2000s they received huge amounts of multilateral and bilateral aid, which, according to an adviser to the former President of Kyrgyzstan, "became the target of large-scale squandering by the political elite."[78]

55%

Proportion of rural households in Tajikistan for which remittances, mostly from the Russian Federation, are the main source of income[79]

Burkina Faso

Burkina Faso is among the 10 poorest countries in the world, with more than half of its people living in extreme poverty. More than one third of Burkinabes are undernourished, and food insecurity is a structural problem. In 2013, 1.8 million people were food insecure and faced little prospect of improvement without fundamental changes to the root causes of their vulnerability.

Changing rainfall patterns (shorter and unpredictable rainy seasons, droughts and floods) have contributed to dramatic shortfalls in food production. This has exacerbated the impact of other factors, such as poor basic services (health, education), bad governance, a high dependency on external markets, demographic growth, high urbanization rates,[80] and (more recently) violence and extremism.

Burkinabe families have been forced to sell their crops, farms and houses in order to pay debts, buy food and cover other basic needs. As a result, households' capacity to cope with future shocks has diminished to a level where even normal times become bad times for the poor. Those without access to land have to rely on local markets, where prices are rising. The arrival of more than 40,000 refugees (and their cattle) fleeing from fighting in Mali has placed more pressure on people who are already highly vulnerable.

1.8 million

Number of people in Burkina Faso who were food insecure in 2013. Many families were putting any surplus from the harvest towards paying back debts incurred during 2012 crisis[81]

Southern Africa

Southern Africa faces a variety of social and environmental hazards, including floods, droughts, food insecurity, political instability and epidemics. It experienced 47 humanitarian emergencies between 2000 and 2012, the majority of which were primarily associated with environmental factors. Twenty-six involved flooding that affected 500,000 people or more. Seven were linked to sociopolitical triggers and three to epidemics.

A legacy of conflict in some countries, e.g. Angola and Mozambique, means large numbers of people are still affected by violence and human-induced emergencies, especially in urban areas. Structural inequalities, chronic malnutrition and HIV/AIDS compound the risk of crisis, and demographic growth is a constant challenge. Southern Africa's population is expected to rise from 167 million in 2012 to 215 million in 2025, with 56 per cent of people in urban areas that lack capacity and infrastructure. Many will live in slums that lack basic services.

In nine of 14 countries, between 20 and 25 per cent of the population is aged between 15 and 24 years. Many are unemployed or underemployed. Regional protocols on free trade and free movement mean that people are becoming increasingly mobile, and transboundary emergencies are becoming more frequent. Global shocks, such as the global food and financial crises of 2007/8, spread easily throughout the region.

26

Number of flood events in Southern Africa that affected more than 500,000 people between 2000 and 2012[82]

Recurrent crises

Children in Niger are at risk of malnutrition due to drought and high food prices. Recurrent crises have hit the Sahel in recent years and 11 million people were affected by food insecurity in 2013. Humanitarian and development organizations are starting to align their work to help families build resilience and manage crisis risk.

CHAPTER 2
Why risk matters to humanitarian assistance

Chapter Takeaways

▶ Managing the risk of crises, rather than simply responding to them when they occur, saves lives and money. Crises can often be predicted and, while their prevention and mitigation is widely supported in theory, it too rarely takes place in practice.

▶ Everyone—from individuals and communities to Governments, humanitarian and development organizations and the private sector— can contribute to managing crisis risk. Risk management is a universal concept that can be applied to all humanitarian crises, although it is context specific, with conflict requiring special consideration.

▶ There are a number of fundamental barriers to implementing a systematic, risk-oriented approach to humanitarian crises. These include: a lack of prioritization by Governments and aid organizations; insufficient support from donors and the public; the disconnect between the work of humanitarian and development organizations; and a system of incentives that does not reward leaders for managing risk.

This chapter describes approaches that contribute to managing crisis risk, and the existing barriers to anticipating and preventing humanitarian crises. It discusses the role of Governments and others, as well as how the humanitarian sector can contribute to better crisis-risk management.

1:4 to 1:36

Cost to benefit ratios of early warning systems[83][84]

Why manage crisis risk?

There are moral, financial, political and practical reasons for managing the risk of humanitarian crises.

- **Moral:** Humanitarian crises cause immense human suffering. There is a moral imperative to prevent and mitigate them as much as possible in order to reduce that suffering.[85] [86] [87]

- **Financial:** It is more cost-effective to manage the risk of crises than to respond to them after they occur. For example, research in Kenya and Ethiopia found that early drought response was around three times more cost-effective than emergency response.[88] [89] Upgrading early warning capacity in developing countries has a cost-to-benefit ratio of between 1:4 and 1:36.[90] [91]

- **Political:** Governments are increasingly held to account for not doing enough to prevent crises. The spread of mobile technology and social media is giving rise to more connected, better-informed people,[92] leading to higher expectations that Governments will prevent and manage crises.[93]

- **Practical:** Aid that takes a long-term view and seeks to manage risk, as well as promotes ownership by people that receive it, is seen as more effective and efficient. It can ultimately have greater impact.[94]

How risk is managed

Managing risk is a systematic process to address uncertainty and ensure the least possible negative consequences (figure 11). It involves the following steps:

Figure 11

Conceptual model of risk management, according to the World Development Report 2014[95]

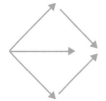

Insurance
To transfer resources across people and over time, from good to bad states of nature

Knowledge
To understand shocks, internal and external conditions, and potential outcomes, thus reducing uncertainty

Coping
To recover from losses and make the most of benefits

Protection
To reduce the probability and size of losses and increase those of benefits

Preparation ⟷ Coping

Preparation for risk consists of three actions that can be taken in advance: acquiring knowledge, building protection, and obtaining insurance. Once a risk (or an opportunity) materializes, people take action to cope with what has occurred. A strong risk management strategy would include all four of these components, which interact and reinforce each other.

"Food crises can often be predicted 6-9 months in advance."

Rob Bailey, Chatham House[96]

Identifying, assessing and monitoring risk

Crises can often be predicted. For example, some food-security crises can be foreseen many months in advance, hurricanes happen every season and specific storms can be anticipated a few days before they strike. Earthquakes cannot be predicted, but the location of seismic risk is known. Conflict is usually accompanied by warning signs. Scientific advances are constantly improving the predictability of hazards (figure 12).[97] The first step is to identify, analyse and monitor risk. Ideally, this will take a multi-hazard approach that includes all potential causes, including natural phenomena, the environment, political stability, health, and financial and economic shocks. It should include a means of assessing the effects of hazards on different people and their varying capacity to cope.

Schematic summary of current and possible future ability to anticipate different hazard types. From Foresight (2012).[98]

Figure 12

| | Ability to produce reliable forecasts | | | | | |
| | Now | | | 2040 | | |
	Spatial	Magnitude	Temporal	Spatial	Magnitude	Temporal
Geophysical hazards						
Earthquakes	2	1	1	3	2	1
Volcanoes	3	2	2	5	3	3
Landslides	2	2	1	3	3	2
Tsunamis	2	2	1	3	3	2
Hydrometeorological hazards	6 days ahead					
Storms	3	3	4	5	5	5
Floods	3	3	4	5	5	5
Droughts	5	5	5	5	5	5
Hydrometeorological hazards	6 months ahead					
Storms	2	2	2	3	3	3
Floods	2	2	2	4	4	4
Droughts	2	2	2	4	4	4
Infectious disease epidemics						
Known Pathogens	2	5	2	4	5	4
Recently emerged pathogens	1	4	1	2	4	2
Pathogens detected in animal reservoirs	1	1	1	2	3	2

1	2	3	4	5
Low ability		Medium ability		High ability

Reducing the potential impact of risks

The potential impact of priority risks can be reduced through land-use planning, infrastructure, natural resource management and enforcing building codes. Vulnerability can be reduced through social protection, basic services, protecting critical infrastructure, diversifying livelihoods and improving community security. In conflict situations, there is prevention and peacebuilding.

Transferring risk

Risk can be transferred or shared. For example, an insurance policy transfers the risk of loss from the policyholder to the insurance company. Catastrophe bonds (securities linked to natural hazards) are an alternative form of insurance. For example, New York City issued a $200 million catastrophe bond following Hurricane Sandy to cover the risk of flooding over the next three years.[99] Risk transfer can also be applied at the individual and community level, for example, through microinsurance or risk mutualization (sharing), such as by drought-affected farmers.

Managing residual risk

When risks cannot be sufficiently reduced in advance, measures need to be implemented to cope with their impact. This might include early warning, preparedness and contingency planning. It might also involve emergency response and recovery, which can contribute to managing future risk by building people's resilience. Emergency response may be the only way to build up resilience while crises are ongoing.

Different contexts, different risks

Risk management is a universal concept that can be applied to all types of humanitarian crises. However, all crises are different and context is paramount.[100] A number of context-specific policy options are identified (figure 13).

Situations of conflict or potential conflict present a unique challenge. Governments may be unwilling to address them and may prevent international partners from doing so. For humanitarian organizations, working to manage conflict risk can be seen as political or social advocacy, with associated threats to neutrality, impartiality and independence. This can undermine trust, which is needed to ensure access to people in need. This dynamic can limit their engagement with Governments and other parties.

Nevertheless, some elements of the risk-management approach can still be applied, such as a comprehensive context analysis, or the shared use of early warning systems. This can go beyond conflict prevention and other political activities. One example is the case of the ethnic clashes in Kyrgyzstan. Multi-hazard analysis and programming might have addressed some of the root causes of discontent (access to clean water, decline of agricultural economy, lack of clarity over grazing rights and poor access to education).

Examples of risk-management options across key policy areas.
From Mitchell and Harris (2012).[101]

Figure 13

	RISK REDUCTION (preventing hazard /shock, reducing exposure and vulnerability)	TRANSFER OR SHARE RISKS	BEING BETTER PREPARED	RESPONDING AND RECOVERING EFFECTIVELY
CLIMATE CHANGE RISK	Greenhouse gas emissions reduction, poverty reduction	(Re)insurance, community savings and other forms of risk pooling	Monitor salinisation, coral bleaching, seasonal forecasts	Support environmental migration and livelihood transitions
DISASTER RISK	Land use planning, poverty reduction, strong building codes with enforcement	(Re)insurance, community savings and other forms of risk pooling	Early warning, evacuation, first aid training	Cash-transfers, rapid shelter provision, risk assessments in reconstruction
CONFLICT RISK	Conflict analysis informing policy and programming decisions, consensus building approaches, electoral reform in some contexts	Building wider allegiances and coalitions for peace	Early warning, conflict analysis, training in mediation, development of negotiation strategies, proactive peacekeeping	Peacekeeping, transitional justice/ peace building, new governance and decision-making processes, economic opportunities
ECONOMIC AND FINANCIAL SHOCKS	Transformative and promotive social protection, land reform, migration, build foreign reserves	Redistributive tax measures, with investment in welfare/ benefit for more exposed individuals	Early warning, economic trend analysis, coordination between government departments, macro-economic shock facilities	Cash and other asset transfers, increases in aid, supported investment flows.

Whose responsibility is it?

People and communities can manage small risks themselves, but the primary responsibility for managing the risk of humanitarian crises lies with Governments. It is their duty to protect the life and security of their citizens, in addition to other human rights.[102] Governments also have legal obligations to prevent, reduce and respond to crises. Under the Hyogo Framework for Action, for example, they commit to "reduce underlying risk factors."[103] The International Law Commission specifies obligations to "prevent harm to one's own population, property and the environment generally."[104]

Risk management is increasingly common practice across all Government functions. For example, Canada's British Colombia Province requires "the integrated and coordinated application of risk management congruently across ministries and public sector agencies, and through each organization, from cabinet, ministry executive, division, branch and work unit, right down to the individual employee providing front line service."[105]

However, in developing countries international support may be required. Economic and social development can reduce and create risk, and risk management needs to be an essential and integrated part of development organizations' work. Humanitarian organizations can also contribute to managing risk, according to their comparative advantage (see below).

The way in which development and humanitarian organizations help Governments to manage risk will vary according to the principles that guide them. For example, the Paris Declaration on Aid Effectiveness stresses national ownership as one of the guiding principles of development.[106] But humanitarian action is based on the principles of neutrality, impartiality and independence,[107] [108] which can limit engagement with Governments even outside of conflict settings. There are also differences in the time frame of engagement: development support is normally planned several years in advance, while humanitarian support operates over a shorter planning cycle.

The role of humanitarian organizations in managing crisis risk

More than 90 per cent of the survey respondents agreed that anticipation and prevention are very or completely important for the humanitarian sector.[109]

There have been many initiatives and approaches related to risk management over the years, but they have taken place in an unsystematic way. The sector has implemented efforts including disaster risk reduction; the "do no harm" approach; early warning and early action; emergency preparedness and contingency planning; early recovery; transition activities; relief, rehabilitation and development; and livelihoods support.

Since the food crises in the Horn of Africa and the Sahel, there has been a renewed interest in building people's resilience to crises. This debate has helped clarify the humanitarian sector's comparative advantage in managing risk, as well as its potential role in and connections with the responsibilities of Governments, the development sector and other actors. Its comparative advantage includes its presence in crisis-affected locations, as well as its speed and flexibility in deploying staff and resources.[110]

91%

Proportion of surveyed experts that think anticipation and prevention of crises is very important for humanitarian organizations

Elements of managing crisis risk under way in the humanitarian sector include:

- **Emergency preparedness**, to ensure international humanitarian agencies can respond quickly and effectively to emergencies, as well as building national and local actors' capacity.

- **Early action**, to mitigate the effects of deteriorating situations and support communities in ways that do not erode their capacity to deal with future risks.

- **Supporting livelihoods**, so that people do not lose everything during crises, and they can continue to support themselves after a shock and become more resilient.

However, these activities are still not systematically embedded in the way the humanitarian system operates as a whole. There is a major shortfall in funding for preparedness, and roles and responsibilities remain unclear. Early recovery, which embodies many concepts of managing risk, has been turned into a discrete "sector" and is consistently underfunded. These and other shortcomings reveal fundamental barriers to implementing a systematic, risk-oriented approach.

What stands in the way of managing crisis risk?

Knowledge without action

According to survey respondents and interviewees, the availability of information is not the main barrier to risk management.[111][112] Over recent years, the humanitarian sector has invested considerable resources in information collection and analysis, including USAID's Famine Early Warning Systems Network (1985), OCHA's information management mandate and capacity (1991) and the Assessment Capacities Project (2009). Humanitarian organizations today have access to an unprecedented amount of data.

Nonetheless, the way in which risk information is communicated and shared needs considerable improvement, especially on conflict-related issues. Humanitarian organizations do not have sufficient capacity to analyse and take decisions on the basis of crisis-risk information in a way that leads to action. Slow responses to the food crises in the Horn of Africa and, to a lesser extent, the Sahel in 2011 are examples of a systemic failure to translate information into action before it is too late.

In the Horn of Africa, early warning was accurate and timely across the region. It prompted some early action in Ethiopia but not in Somalia and Kenya. In these countries, neither of the humanitarian country teams managed to develop serious scenario or contingency planning for a major crisis, or effective early action programmes. Their leadership was biased towards information sharing and consensus instead of strategic coherence and firm decisions.[113][114]

A matter of priorities

If information is not the main barrier to managing crisis risk, what is? Survey respondents identified "insufficient resources or capacity,", "insufficient interest by donors and the general public", "insufficient cooperation with non-humanitarian actors" and "insufficient focus on prevention by humanitarian organizations" (figure 14). Organizational culture was also seen as important.

Experts surveyed and interviewed for this report suggested that institutional, organizational, financial and cultural barriers were preventing a more systematic approach to crisis management. In particular, they felt that insufficient donor interest meant that managing crisis risk was not being prioritized by their organizations or part of their ethos.

The following sections explore the possible reasons for this.

"Most disasters or crises can be predicted. In this day and age, there are enough indicators and data, and enough coverage by Governments and NGOs to know when things are looking bad or likely will be bad. And so we should be able to intervene to stop it."

Sarah Lumsdon, Oxfam[115]

Figure 14

Barriers to anticipating and preventing humanitarian crises by level of importance

Question: What do you think are the main factors that limit humanitarian organizations from anticipating and preventing humanitarian crises? Please rate them by level of importance

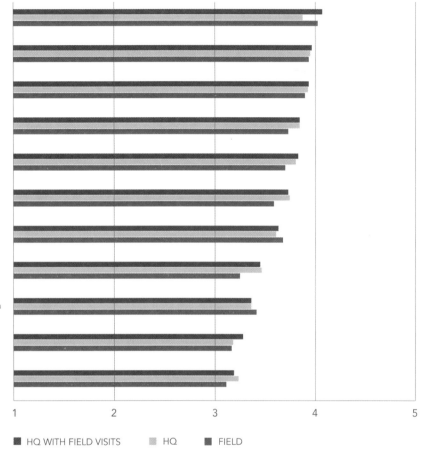

Insufficient resources or capacity to work on prevention

Insufficient interest by donors and the general public

Insufficient cooperation with non-humanitarian actors

Insufficient programmatic focus on prevention in central humanitarian organizations

Insufficient cooperation among humanitarian organizations

Organizational culture

Insufficient resources or capacity to analyze information

No single agency with clear role and mandate for prevention

Insufficient time to analyze information

Insufficient access to relevant information

Information is too complex to understand

■ HQ WITH FIELD VISITS   ■ HQ   ■ FIELD

Insufficient donor and public support

Donors shape the international response system by the way they fund.[116] Some recent donor initiatives have shown an increasing focus on anticipation. For example, the UK, US and EU led efforts around resilience, and Australia provided significant funding for disaster preparedness. However, only 4.7 per cent of total humanitarian funding and 0.7 per cent of development spending goes to disaster preparedness and prevention.[117]

DARA's Humanitarian Response Index, which measures how well OECD/DAC donors abide by the Good Humanitarian Donorship principles, reveals a persistent lack of political commitment to risk management. Donor Governments score 30 per cent lower on prevention, risk reduction and recovery indicators than on other components of their aid.[118]

For many, this lack of interest can be attributed to politics and the need for Governments to demonstrate quick, dramatic results to their constituents. Other explanations include strict legislation, the number and magnitude of emergencies requiring response, and the separation of donor agencies addressing humanitarian and development assistance. Some donors may also lack confidence in humanitarian organizations' capacity to do the job.

Funding decisions can often be best understood as political.[119] Geopolitics may play in favour of or against early action, depending on how donor Governments understand the interplay between humanitarian risks and their security, economic or political interests.[120]

The focus on emergency response rather than prevention is also related to public awareness. The media, particularly television, exert a strong influence on the decisions and foreign-policy agendas of Western Governments, and they tend to focus on crises only when they have reached a high level of suffering.

Nonetheless, funding decisions relating to prevention and mitigation are often made in the relevant ministries before the public is even aware of a crisis. The issue here becomes less one of media management than how to raise the profile of a potential emergency among technical and political officials.

This applies not only to donor countries but also to Government recipients of humanitarian assistance. Where affected Governments have taken the lead in managing crisis risk (such as Indonesia and Niger), donor funding often follows.

"The responses to crises like the Haiti earthquake, Pakistan floods or drought and famine in the Horn of Africa show the human consequences of a lack of sustained commitment by donor governments for prevention, preparedness, risk reduction and long-term recovery efforts."

DARA Humanitarian Response Index[121]

"Humanitarian and development groups should co-ordinate more. There is a disconnect between decision makers for development and humanitarian groups."

Maria Kiani, HAP International[122]

The humanitarian and development divide

Another barrier to anticipation and prevention is the institutional separation between humanitarian and development work in terms of analysis, planning, programming and funding. This applies to humanitarian organizations, recipients and donor Governments.

Paradoxically, most humanitarian organizations undertake humanitarian and development programming, and the humanitarian departments of many donor Governments belong to development agencies. Six out of the top 10 recipient countries of Official Development Assistance according to the World Bank (Afghanistan, Ethiopia, Democratic Republic of the Congo, Kenya, occupied Palestinian territories and Pakistan) are also major recipients of humanitarian aid.

Nonetheless, there is a disconnect between humanitarian and development work, with several negative consequences. Useful information and risk analysis are not shared, and there is insufficient joint planning to ensure a comprehensive and coherent approach to risk.

The humanitarian-development divide creates a gap between short-term humanitarian programmes (often one year) and long-term development (five or more years). It inhibits medium-term activities (e.g. disaster preparedness, safety nets, livelihoods support)

that could prevent crises and support recovery. When there is the threat of a humanitarian crisis, development funding may be too inflexible to prevent it; once a crisis takes hold, development funding may not be available.

This divide has been discussed for many years, and some efforts have been made to address it. For example, the UN's High-Level Task Force (HLTF) on Food Security, established after the food crisis in 2007/8, brought together many actors to coordinate the response, and it simultaneously addressed immediate needs and the underlying causes of food insecurity.[123] Responsibilities were divided according to agencies' expertise, not according to whether they were humanitarian or development. An evaluation of the HLTF in 2013 found that it had played an important role in "changing the global narrative about food security" and "setting the stage for improved policy coherence."[124]

This approach has yet to be translated into better operations at the country level, but attempts are being made. For example, the UN has developed an integrated regional strategy for the Sahel, which brings together security, development and humanitarian objectives.[125] OCHA and UNDP, supported by the UK-led Political Champions for Disaster Resilience, are exploring ways to align humanitarian and development work through a series of pilot projects.[126]

In countries where the UN has a Country Team and a multidimensional peacekeeping or political mission, it undertakes integrated analysis and planning through a task force. This brings together different offices and agencies of the UN at headquarters and at country level to develop a shared vision of the UN's strategic objectives and undertake closely aligned or integrated planning. However, there currently is no equivalent for humanitarian and development work.

A lack of risk-focused leadership

Managing crisis risk requires joint and coordinated efforts. However, more than 20 years after UN resolution 46/182,[127] which created today's mechanisms for coordination in the international humanitarian system, the sector is failing to go beyond emergency response.

Evaluations reveal a lack of attention to activities that contribute to managing risk. Accountability for such activities is weak within organizations and coordination structures, and budgeting and planning do not reflect a strategic approach to crisis prevention and management. Managers are not held to account for failing to share information, or for declining to take a strategic approach to risk.[128] [129 130 131]

Many assign these failures to humanitarian coordination and leadership. The common technical, coordination and funding tools introduced by recent reforms have failed to support anticipation and risk management.[132] Competition for funds fosters agency allegiance over system-wide loyalty, and staff commitment to coordinated outcomes is neither required nor rewarded.[133]

Leaders are not shifting the vision of their organizations towards a risk-management approach. According to one interviewee: "Actually, very few people are in a position to change things. It is all about these people measuring success differently."

Supporting risk management requires clear messages from headquarters (transformative leadership) and a detailed road map for teams in the field (operational leadership).[134] UN agencies and many international NGOs have managerial, rather than results-driven, approaches, further inhibiting the leadership needed to address crisis risks.

Translating support into action

This study has found strong support among humanitarian experts for a humanitarian sector that contributes to crisis anticipation, prevention, management and recovery. This should be linked with similar efforts by Governments and the development sector. Efforts exist to make this happen, but they are unsystematic and there are major barriers that prevent this from becoming a reality.

What is needed to make a risk-oriented approach to humanitarian crises a reality? According to experts interviewed for this report, the following elements are crucial:

• Prioritization of crisis-risk management by Governments, the development sector and humanitarian organizations.

• Joint initiatives to analyse and prioritize risks, joint planning, and agreement on what risks will be managed by whom.

• Programming, especially outside of acute crises, that includes early action, preparedness, livelihoods support and resilience-building, and which uses a wider range of ways to manage and share risk, such as insurance.

• Predictable, flexible financing.

• Strong leadership and advocacy at the national and global level.

Chapter 3 explores this vision further.

"New risk management cultures, with new incentive and accountability frameworks, must be developed. This demands strong and concerted leadership from senior managers in agencies and donors who must communicate a sustained vision to their staff and explain and justify the changes to be made."

Managing Famine Risk: Linking Early Warning to Early Action[135]

Adapting to new risks

Farmers in Lesotho being trained in seed production of drought tolerant crops. The impact of climate change is affecting Lesotho's progress towards development. This project, implemented by several UN agencies, is using locally-led efforts to support people affected by drought so they can sustain minimum living standards in the face of new risks.

CHAPTER 3
Managing crisis risk more effectively

Chapter Takeaways

▶ Prioritization of crisis-risk management and collaboration between Governments, humanitarian organizations and development agencies is essential to prevent and reduce the impact of future crises. This involves: building national and local capacity to manage risk; clarifying roles and responsibilities; working more closely together; and ensuring managing crisis risk is part of national and global development frameworks, including the post-2015 development agenda.

▶ There are many existing positive examples of good practices that can help manage the risk of humanitarian crises. However, they are generally ad hoc and not part of a systematic approach to how Governments and aid organizations work. The types of programming that can help communities manage risk already exist and need to be scaled up.

▶ Planning based on a shared and comprehensive analysis of risk allows all actors to effectively address risks before they become crises. Appropriate tools and processes are needed to support this and the planning cycles of humanitarian and development organizations need to be more closely aligned.

▶ Funding for managing crisis risk is inadequate and poorly targeted. Basing funding on an objective and shared risk assessment would help prioritize funding flows and promote better coordination among donors. Many funding mechanisms already exist to channel funds, although they may require adaptations. Insurance and other risk-sharing mechanisms can be an important part of the solution.

▶ Strong leadership is needed to foster a risk-oriented approach to humanitarian crises. This applies at global, national and organizational level. Advocacy is equally important and the post-2015 development agenda and the World Humanitarian Summit in 2016 offer good opportunities for joint advocacy on crisis-risk management.

Many humanitarian initiatives already contribute to managing crisis risk. This chapter draws on examples to explore how humanitarian organizations can maximize their contributions and work more closely with Governments and development agencies. It highlights best practices and opportunities for change across four key areas:

1. Linking Government, development and humanitarian efforts

2. Analysis, planning and programming

3. Funding a crisis-risk management approach

4. Leadership and advocacy

The end of each section contains a summary of recommendations.

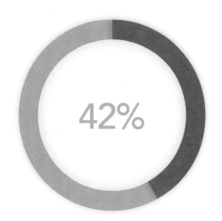

42%

Reduction in economic growth rate (from 12% to 7%) after the 2000 floods in Mozambique[138]

Linking Government, development and humanitarian efforts

Collaboration between Governments, humanitarian organizations and development agencies is essential to prevent and reduce the impact of crises. This is especially the case in protracted emergencies, and where people face the prospect of major disasters every year.

Raising the profile of risk management in Government

Recent dramatic events, including unprecedented natural disasters, the global recession and the Arab spring, have demonstrated the fallibility of long-accepted economic models and political assumptions.[136] Managing crisis risk can save lives, avert economic damage, prevent development setbacks and unleash new opportunities.[137]

Mozambique, for example, faces a long-term challenge with floods, cyclones and drought. Its floods in 2000 were some of the costliest

disasters in its history. At least 700 people died, 650,000 were displaced and economic growth rates decreased from 12 to 7 per cent.[139]

Since then, new structures have been implemented to manage and mitigate disasters. In 1999, Mozambique passed a National Policy on Disaster Management and created a National Disaster Management Institute. It develops a master plan for disaster prevention and mitigation every five years, with a dedicated budget. The Prime Minister leads coordination, and every institution and ministry is required to integrate risk reduction into its planning.

These initiatives have had real impact in terms of lives saved. After Tropical Cyclone Funso hit Mozambique in 2012, only 40 deaths were reported—much lower than during the floods of 2000 and 2001.[140]

When a Government takes the lead, it can improve links between humanitarian and development organizations, multiplying their efforts. In Niger, the Government-led 3N initiative—Les Nigériens Nourissent les Nigériens—set short- and long-term priorities for addressing food insecurity, which partners could rally around.[141]

Results of the UK National Risk Register of Civil Emergencies 2013. Risks are prioritized by likelihood and potential impact. Note the figure does not show risks of terrorist and other malicious attacks. From UK Government (2013).[142]

Figure 15

SEVERITY ▼

	BETWEEN 1 IN 20.000 AND 1 IN 2.000	BETWEEN 1 IN 2.000 AND 1 IN 200	BETWEEN 1 IN 200 AND 1 IN 20	BETWEEN 1 IN 20 AND 1 IN 2	GREATER THAN 1 IN 2
5				• Pandemic influenza	
4			• Coastal flooding • Effusive volcanic eruption		
3	• Major transport accidents	• Major industrial accidents	• Other infectious diseases • IInland flooding	• Severe space weather • Low temperatures and heavy snow • Heatwaves	
2			• Animal diseases • Drought • Public disorder	• Explosive volcanic eruption • Storms and gales	
1			• Severe wildfires	• Disruptive industrial action	

Relative likelihood of occurring in the next five years

The Nigerien National Dispositive provided a platform for the Government, operational agencies and donors to determine early response actions and mobilize resources after food-insecurity warnings in 2011. This enabled a timely response that saved lives and averted a major catastrophe.[143] It also led to efficiencies and saved money, notably through interventions in the three months after the harvest, when food prices were lower and households could choose from a wider set of economic options. This was in contrast to the costly late response of 2010.[144]

Some countries are taking risk management even further by introducing a comprehensive risk-management framework. The UK and the Netherlands have introduced national risk assessments to improve prevention of and planning for crises.[145][146] They both take similar approaches: identify risks, generate scenarios, and assess the probability, impact, and therefore priority, of risks (figure 15). This helps coordination and cooperation across ministries and organizations, helps to avoid conflicts between stakeholders during a crisis, and involves other actors, such as the private sector.[147]

Building national and local capacity to manage risk

To manage the risk of crises over the long term, national and local actors need the capacity to take the lead. As a senior humanitarian official working in South-East Asia asserted: "The first responsibility to manage risks lies in the host country. Building local capacity is the right approach."

Some international initiatives seek to encourage this. The IASC/UNDG/UNISDR Common Framework for Capacity Development for Preparedness brings together development and humanitarian organizations in one process to support Governments. However, it has a narrow focus on emergency

"[International organizations] have good techniques but are weak in mobilizing the community people, since they have limited time-frame. Not all people from the community know well about the organization and its purpose. Since they cannot build the capacity of the community people, the projects are not sustainable."

Local man, Myanmar[148]

preparedness, and there are no equivalents for other areas of risk management, such as risk analysis.[149]

Helping local communities manage risk is also critical.[150] This requires Governments, donors and international organizations to support early warning systems at the community level,[151] and to improve community access to official early warning information.[152] Mobile technology and social media, combined with Government open-data policies, provide new opportunities to do this.[153]

Partners for Resilience is one initiative working on local capacity for managing crisis risk. It has a list of minimum standards to help communities reduce climate risks with limited external support,[154] and it is helping them reach those standards. They include being able to interpret early warnings about possible climatic shocks, conducting and updating risk assessments, and identifying ways to adapt or change their livelihoods. The community should also have relationships with meteorological agencies and communicate their needs to Government officials.[155]

How humanitarian organizations can help Governments manage risk

Humanitarian organizations are already working with Governments to build their capacity to manage crisis risk. For example, OCHA helped Indonesia set up an institutional and legal framework for disaster management. In Kyrgyzstan, the French NGO ACTED helped the Government improve its monitoring of natural hazards and developed a tool to assess all types of risks, including conflict, which international and national organizations now use.

However, the role of humanitarian organizations is often not formalised or systematic. If humanitarian organizations want to contribute to managing crisis risk, they need to identify their role based on competence and comparative advantage, and offer services aligned with the priorities and work of their partners.

"AGIR starts from the premise that while emergency response is crucial to saving lives, the time has come for a sustained effort to help people in the Sahel cope better with recurrent crises, with a particular effort towards the most vulnerable people."

Objectives of The Global Alliance for Resilience (AGIR)

For example, the European Commission Directorate-General for Humanitarian Aid and Civil Protection (ECHO) has identified its role in risk reduction and resilience. This includes advocacy in its development work and ensuring its humanitarian assistance systematically addresses risk. This clarity has resulted in more effective humanitarian action and is helping to ensure that development aid addresses crisis risk.[156]

Declaring a crisis is the primary method for Governments to request humanitarian assistance, and they may face sensitivities when doing so. When the earliest warning signals appear, Governments may be unwilling to declare a crisis for fear of how such a request may be perceived domestically or by international development partners.

There are limited options for Governments to reliably seek humanitarian agencies' support outside of acute crises, which is when support to manage risk could be most useful. This is because humanitarian organizations and donors, as well as the tools they use, respond mainly to crises and needs that already exist rather than potential future ones.

OCHA's Regional Office for Asia and the Pacific addressed these issues by publishing a guide that shows national disaster managers how to use international tools and services. It also helps them to locate international technical expertise before a disaster.[157]

Collaboration initiatives

Many initiatives seek to encourage greater collaboration between humanitarian and development organizations, particularly those relating to disaster risk reduction (DRR).[158] These include the Hyogo Framework for Action (HFA) and the UN Plan of Action on Disaster Risk Reduction for Resilience.[159] [160]

In 2012, ECOWAS and the EU developed an initiative to bridge the gap between emergency response and development, with a focus on food security. The Global Alliance for Resilience Initiative—known as AGIR—brings together more than 30 country representatives, humanitarian and development organizations, and regional bodies.[161]

As a result, many countries in the Sahel have started to identify national resilience priorities, and donors have realigned their long-term support around them, such as by supporting a regional food-reserve project. It has improved the links between humanitarian response and development assistance, and inspired closer cooperation among technical and financial partners at the country level.[162]

CADRI is a global inter-agency initiative to build capacity for DRR.[163] Originally it brought together UNDP, OCHA and UNISDR, but its membership is expanding.[164] However, according to a recent evaluation, it has experienced difficulties due to limited commitment from member agencies and an absence of leadership.[165] Many interviewees noted that such initiatives often reach a dead end due to a lack of support, direction and leadership from headquarters. If these initiatives are to succeed, participating agencies must dedicate staff time and resources to them, and include them in their strategic and financial plans.

Crisis-risk management and the post-2015 development framework

Over the last 20 years, the global community has come together around two historic development efforts: Agenda 21 on sustainable development, and the Millennium Development Goals (MDGs) on poverty eradication.[166 167] The MDG initiative ends in

$38 trillion

Cost of disasters to the global economy between 1980 and 2012. Equivalent to half the value of the world economy in 2013[168]

2015, and Governments are discussing its successor.[169]

This post-2015 development framework will include the successor to the HFA on DRR,[170] and it represents a once-in-a-generation opportunity to incorporate crisis-risk management into future development frameworks.

Crises can cancel progress on poverty reduction.[171] For example, Rizal Province in the Philippines saw poverty almost double after it was struck by Tropical Storm Ondoy and Typhoon Pepeng in 2009. Even today, the incidence is higher than before the storms.[172] Typhoon Haiyan, which hit one of the Philippines' poorest areas, is likely to have a similar impact. Disasters cost the global economy $38 trillion between 1980 and 2012.[173]

The MDGs and HFA were based on the paradigm that crises and disasters are discrete events, separate from the development process. They were seen as external and unforeseen shocks that affect normally functioning economies and societies, rather than as indicators of failed development, or unsustainable social and economic processes. This led to crisis-risk management approaches that were autonomous from mainstream development concerns, such as economic growth and infrastructure.

To save lives in humanitarian crises and reach global aspirations to end extreme poverty and promote shared prosperity, crisis-risk management needs to be integrated in the

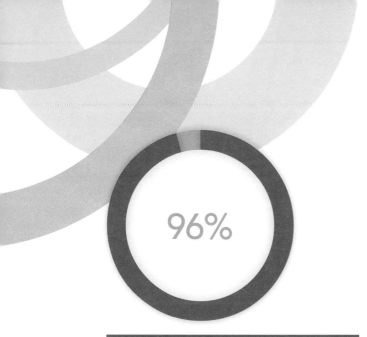

96%

Proportion of OCHA's surge deployments in Asia-Pacific over a five-year period that could have been predicted by risk modelling[174]

post-2015 development agenda.[175] For this to happen, it must address the role of risk and crises in undermining development, and include a specific target to reduce risk and incorporate risk management across other relevant goals. It needs to ensure that development adequately targets the countries and people most vulnerable to disaster and crisis.[176]

Recommendations

- Governments should prioritize crisis-risk management in order to prevent and mitigate future humanitarian crises. They should address the underlying drivers of risk through all Government functions; provide livelihood options, basic services and social protection for the most vulnerable people; and set up systems for crisis anticipation, preparedness and response.

- Humanitarian organizations should increase and formalize their role in managing the risk of crises, work more closely with Governments to build national and local capacity, and provide aid that meets immediate needs and addresses future risk.

- Humanitarian and development organizations should support existing and develop new joint initiatives that contribute to crisis anticipation, prevention, mitigation and recovery. They should also make long-term commitments of resources to those initiatives.

- Governments should ensure that development aid targets the people and countries most at risk from humanitarian crises. Crisis risk management should be fully integrated into national development plans, bilateral framework agreements and specifically included in the post-2015 development agenda.

Analysis, planning and programming

The program cycle—analyzing needs, strategic planning, mobilizing resources and implementing assistance programmes—is at the core of humanitarian aid. This section examines how humanitarian analysis planning and programming could be adjusted to improve crisis-risk management. In particular, it highlights the value of shared analysis and planning processes around common objectives between humanitarian and development organizations.

Risk analysis

Risk analysis is necessary to identify and prioritize the people and places most likely to experience humanitarian crises. It should be carried out at national and local levels, and include not only the assessment of all hazards, but also of people's vulnerability and their capacity to deal with shocks. "Vulnerability and capacity assessment" looks at the drivers that lead to risks becoming crises, as well as the resources a community has to cope with the consequences.[177]

In Kyrgyzstan, ACTED developed REACH—a multi-hazard, community-based risk-analysis tool.[178] It combines social and economic data from sources such as the Kyrgyz Government and the World Bank, WFP's price-monitoring and food-security assessment, natural-hazard information, and ACTED's community risk assessments and dispute analyses. REACH was instrumental in the revision of the humanitarian appeal after the ethnic clashes in 2010.[179]

It is vital that communities take part in risk analysis. In Yemen, the Red Crescent Society carried out a participatory risk analysis in two districts badly affected by flash floods. It revealed that over the previous 15 years, more people had been killed in road accidents than by flooding. Therefore, the society started a road-safety programme designed to reduce accidents, especially near schools, which was widely appreciated.[180]

At the global and national levels, risk-analysis tools can develop a shared understanding of risk so that all actors can target their resources in a coordinated and effective manner. However, most tools focus on specific sectors, rather than taking a comprehensive approach. Furthermore, organizations often develop their internal tools using independent analysis that is often not shared.

To address these problems, a group of UN agencies, donors and research institutions is developing an open and transparent index to identify countries likely to require international assistance in a humanitarian crisis.[181] The Index for Risk Management (InfoRM) model takes a multi-hazard approach and includes vulnerability

"The wisdom of the crowd, the knowledge of experts and the power of algorithms to enable… smarter decisions to solve complex human problems."

Hunchworks[182]

and capacity (figure 16). Earlier versions of the tool predicted 96 per cent of OCHA's surge deployments in the Asia-Pacific region over a five-year period.[183] The initiative intends to develop the methodology at the sub-national level. OECD is also working on a methodology for analysing and measuring resilience.

Developing tools for shared risk analysis is only one part of the solution. Even more important are the processes around them for achieving a common risk assessment.

Climate Outlook Fora is one example of this model. It brings together climate experts and decision makers to analyse seasonal predictions and discuss response options, and to ensure consistency in the way information is accessed and interpreted. Participants assess the likely implications on socioeconomic sectors (e.g. agriculture and water) and base plans on the same information. According to WMO, the forums have "significantly contributed to adaptation to climate variability."[184]

New technologies can support joint risk analysis and consensus-building. HunchWorks, a Global Pulse initiative, is a social network that combines "the wisdom of the crowd, the knowledge of experts and the power of algorithms to enable you to make smarter decisions to solve complex human problems."[185] Users can collect and share information on potential risks. This information is then discussed, complemented by others

Conceptual outline of the Index for Risk Management (InfoRM). From De Groeve et al (2013).[186]

Figure 16

Ranking level	InfoRM					
Concept level	Hazard & Exposure		Vulnerability		Lack of coping capacity	
Functional level	Natural	Human	Socio-economic	Vulnerable groups	Institutional	Infrastructure
Component level	Earthquake Tsunami Flood Tropical cyclone Drought	Conflict intensity Regime instability Extrajudicial and unlawful killings	Development & Deprivation Inequality Aid dependency	Uprooted people Other vulnerable groups	DRR Governance	Communication Physical infrastructure Access to health system

and validated or "trusted," resulting in a final confidence score.

Humanitarian assistance is typically carried out on the basis of assessing people's needs during a crisis. In protracted crises or situations of chronic vulnerability, a lack of a systematic risk analysis may mean that assistance does not lead to long-term improvement. The introduction of the humanitarian needs overview into the programme cycle promotes a more strategic approach. However, humanitarian organizations may need to think further about how they can include risk analysis in the programme cycle.[187]

"I acted as soon as I heard the early warnings. That was the day before the cyclone was supposed to make landfall, but I went anyway. I didn't want to risk anything."

Kamala from Odisha,
India after Cyclone Phailin[188]

Early warning

To be effective, early warning systems must include four elements: knowledge of the risks faced, technical monitoring and warning, dissemination of meaningful warnings to people at risk, and public awareness and preparedness to act.[189] When these elements are in place, early warning systems have reduced the impact of many types of hazards. They have been highly cost-effective, with benefits between four and 36 times their cost.[190]

However, in 2006 UNISDR found major gaps in the world's early warning systems. Despite progress since then, many gaps remain.[191] Systems are often sector specific, such as WFP's Food Security Monitoring System in Tajikistan. Distributed capacity may require separate early warning systems, but all hazards need to be adequately covered, and information should be consolidated and shared more widely.

Risk assessments tend to ignore conflict and political risk due to Government sensitivity and the operational challenges of predicting conflict. There is currently no UN conflict early warning system, despite calls for its development by the Secretary-General and the UN Security Council in 2011.[192][193] Where sophisticated conflict early warning systems do exist, they are usually either classified or highly expensive, limiting the information available to humanitarian organizations. Technologies such as machine learning (systems that learn from data they process) are expanding the possibilities for low-cost conflict early warning.[194] However, lack of access to conflict early warning systems remains a serious gap.

From information to action: the role of triggers

Humanitarian organizations often struggle to convert information into action. At the end of the last decade, for example, an effective famine early warning system existed in Somalia, and in 2009 the alarm was sounded. But swift action did not follow, and between October 2010 and April 2012 famine and food insecurity killed 258,000 people, making it one of the deadliest emergencies in decades.[195]

Systems such as the Famine Early Warning Systems Network, or the WHO Global Alert and Response System, generally do not specify when or what action should be taken. The lack of response analysis was a major factor in the late response to the Somalia famine.[196] Many actors, including DFID, have resolved to develop pre-agreed triggers for action,[197] including thresholds in indicators for specific actions. But this has been an onerous and divisive process, with little results.

One barrier is the expectation that triggers must provide a perfect answer. But triggers are simply tools in the risk analysis and planning process. Triggers do not need to automatically initiate a response programme (although they can if part of a wider, proactive risk-management strategy).[198] They can lead to other actions, such as convening key organizations to plan for an emerging situation,

258,000

Number of people killed by famine and food insecurity in Somalia between October 2010 and April 2012. Late response to early warnings contributed to the crisis.[199]

or making surge-capacity deployments of staff and resources. The process of developing and monitoring triggers can improve risk awareness.

Planning for crisis-risk management

In 2012, the Sendai Dialogue examined the lessons of the 2011 Japan earthquake and tsunami. During the event, world leaders called for a more systematic integration of risk management into development planning.[200] However, this is not the case in common practice.

Under the UN system, national development plans are complemented by a Common Country Assessment (analysis), a UN Development Assistance Framework (strategic framework) and Poverty Reduction Strategy Papers, which describe countries' development policies and external financing needs.[201] When a humanitarian crisis requires international support from more than one agency, a Strategic Response Plan (SRP) is prepared.[202] Humanitarian assistance generally follows a one-year planning-and-funding cycle, whereas development planning is longer term.

"To many [local] people, international assistance was seen as a series of disjointed, one-off efforts to meet isolated needs, provided in ways that left incomplete, unsustainable results, rather than holistic interventions that made a long-term impact. Many people talked about how the short-term nature of many aid projects was a major challenge to making projects sustainable."

Listening Project Report Kenya[203]

Aligning these planning processes offers an opportunity to comprehensively manage risk. With a shared risk analysis and priorities, humanitarian and development actors could address different components of those risks and strengthen links between programmes. For example, in a cholera crisis, humanitarian organizations could train and equip medical staff, while development organizations could build better water infrastructure and increase the health system's capacity.

USAID created joint planning cells to bring together relief and development teams to coordinate their programmes by jointly analysing risk and developing common objectives. The team prepares a strategic plan, which sets out how to "layer, integrate and sequence" humanitarian and development assistance.[204] UN agencies also plan jointly in some countries. In Somalia, WFP, UNICEF and FAO developed a joint multi-year and comprehensive strategy for improving resilience.[205] These agencies point out that significant institutional investment and commitment are required to make it work.[206]

A lack of medium-term (one to five years) planning is a significant barrier to crisis-risk management. Currently, humanitarian organizations usually plan for one year ahead, even in places where they have been present for decades. Development plans often look much further ahead. This binary approach inhibits implementing programmes that link the short and long term, which could build people's resilience.[207]

Humanitarian organizations have introduced multi-year SRPs in some countries. South Sudan and countries in the Sahel region will have a three-year plan from 2014.[208] Chad and Somalia introduced longer-term plans for 2013 to 2015.[209] These plans include responses to address immediate emergency priorities, as well as medium- to longer-term requirements, and focus on resilience.[210][211]

Programming for crisis-risk management

Humanitarian programming is overwhelmingly focused on emergency response—the provision of material (food, water, shelter and health care) or logistical assistance. This applies even in places where crisis has become normal. Assistance to prevent and mitigate crisis remains poorly funded and under-represented in humanitarian and development plans.[212]

Activities that can help manage crisis risk include emergency preparedness, early crisis response, livelihood support and diversification, malnutrition prevention, DRR, climate adaptation, social protection, natural resource management (water, land, environmental), provision of basic services, and conflict prevention and peacebuilding (figure 17).[213]

Building communities' capacity to manage risk is also important. For example, Oxfam worked with local NGOs in Indonesia to increase villagers' preparedness for natural hazards. People covered by the project showed greater knowledge of disaster preparedness plans, and they were much more involved in disaster preparedness.[214] Some villages set up volunteer teams to analyse risks and take preventative action, such as cleaning river beds, planting trees and training villagers in first aid.[215]

The best programming addresses risk in a holistic way, covering immediate needs and elements to reduce, transfer and share risk over the longer term. For example, the Rural Resilience Initiative in Ethiopia and Senegal stimulates rural development through a holistic approach that reduces risks through adaptation activities (improving natural resource management); transfers risk through insurance schemes; encourages productive risk-taking to increase production (credit); and encourages and supports saving to help households build sustainable and resilient livelihoods.

Cash-transfer programming and social safety nets

Social-protection programmes, specifically cash-transfer programmes, are a way to manage risk through humanitarian response. They can simultaneously meet people's immediate needs and increase their ability to withstand shocks by building their asset base and allowing them to invest in productive livelihoods.[216]

In 2010, Jeunesse En Mission Entraide et Développement developed an integrated programme in Abalak, northern Niger, that integrates cash for work, cut-price food and fodder, and long-term development activities, including land regeneration and establishing grain banks. This gave households a flexible way to meet their immediate needs while enhancing long-term food security and economic sustainability.[217]

"Humanitarian assistance will seek more opportunities to reduce vulnerability and lay the foundation for longer-term development while continuing its primary focus on saving lives. Development assistance will undertake longer-term programming in chronically vulnerable communities and be sufficiently flexible in higher-risk areas to build resilience and facilitate inclusive growth."

Building Resilience to Recurrent Crisis, USAID

Increasing cash programming provides another opportunity for humanitarian assistance to increase its contribution to crisis-risk management. It provides people with desperately needed money, reducing their need to sell assets, and can stimulate the local economy. WFP aims to use cash for 30 to 40 per cent of all programming by 2015.[218]

Critically, cash transfers can be linked with long-term, national social-protection mechanisms, such as Ethiopia's Productive Safety Net Programme and Kenya's Hunger Safety Net Programme. However, the mechanism for aligning short-term cash responses with long-term programmes needs to be further explored.[220]

30 – 40%

Expected proportion of WFP aid delivered through cash and vouchers by 2015[219]

Recommendations

- Humanitarian and development organizations and donors should base their planning on a common analysis of risk and align their planning cycles where possible. They should support tools and processes to jointly analyse crisis risk, such as the InfoRM initiative. Multi-mandated organizations and donors should strengthen links between their humanitarian and development teams, for example through joint planning cells.

- Where one does not exist, Governments and partners should establish a national coordination forum to jointly analyse and address risks, monitor and share early warning information, and develop triggers for action. Humanitarian organizations may need to establish similar, independent processes in conflict situations.

- Humanitarian organizations should increase the length of their planning cycle to three years in protracted crises. They should increase their use of programmatic approaches–including preparedness, livelihood support and cash-transfer programming–to help communities manage the risk of crises.

Examples of activities that contribute to managing the risk of humanitarian crises from Practical Action's "Vulnerability to Resilience (V2R)" framework. From Practical Action (2011).[221]

Figure 17

Future Uncertainty
Long Term Trends including Climate Change
ADAPTIVE CAPACITY
- Improving understanding of trends & their local impacts
- Ensuring access to relevant & timely information
- Building confidence & flexibility to learn & experiment

Hazards and stresses
DISASTER PREPAREDNESS
- Building capacity to analyze hazards & stresses
- Improving hazard prevention & protection
- Increasing early warning & awareness
- Establishing contingency & emergency planning
- Building back better

Livelihoods
DISASTER & SECURITY
- Strengthening community organization & voice
- Supporting access to & sustainable management of productive assets
- Promoting access to technologies
- Improving access to markets and employment
- Ensuring secure living conditions

RESILIENCE
Ability to manage risk
Ability to adapt to change
Ability to secure sufficient food

Governance
ENABLING ENVIRONMENT
- Centralized & participatory decision-making
- Strengthening links between local, district & national levels
- Promoting integrated approaches to livelihoods, disasters & climate change
- Addressing underlying systemic issues

Funding a crisis-risk management approach

Aid financing affects aid organizations' behaviour and priorities, with consequences that go far beyond its immediate goals. This section looks at improving funding for crisis-risk management, with a specific focus on humanitarian aid.

Spending that can contribute to crisis-risk management is spread across many areas of aid (figure 18), including DRR, climate adaptation, resilience and crisis response. It comes from many sources and flows through a number of funding mechanisms (figure 19).

"For over 40 years, the supply of food relief to my community has been routine, whether it rains or not. Periodic droughts, massive losses of animals and frequent conflicts in this region are being used to justify heavy spending [on] emergency food relief. But [food relief] is not the only way to help a community."

Demo Hassan, livestock trader from Garba Tula, Northern Kenya[222]

Conceptual areas of aid that include spending on crisis-risk management.
From Kellett and Peters (2014).[223]

Figure 18

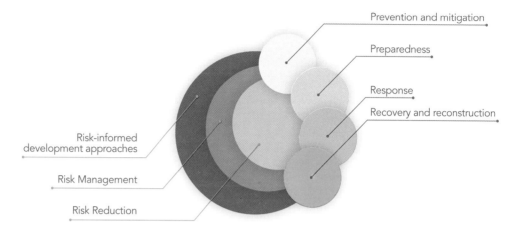

Prevention and mitigation

Preparedness

Response

Recovery and reconstruction

Risk-informed
development approaches

Risk Management

Risk Reduction

Examples of funding sources and tools for crisis-risk management

Figure 19

National budget

Bilateral development assistance

Bilateral humanitarian assistance

Mulitlateral funding

Remittances

Private sector

Climate change funds

UNDP Thematic Trust Fund for Crisis
Prevention and Recovery (CPR TTF)

Climate adaptation mechanisms
(LDC Fund, Adaptation Fund etc.)

World Bank Global Facility for Disaster
Reduction and Recovery (GFDRR)

Humanitarian Pooled funds
(CERF, 5 CHFs, and 13 ERFs in 2013)

UN Consolidated Appeals
and other humanitarian appeals

Stabilization funds

Moving donor funding to a risk-management model

Donors have made collective and individual commitments to increase spending on managing crisis risk. For example, participants at the 2011 Global Platform for Disaster Reduction recommended that DRR should constitute at least 1 per cent of all development funding and 10 per cent of humanitarian funding.[224] However, the reality has fallen short of this ideal.

A lack of conceptual clarity over crisis anticipation, prevention, mitigation and recovery makes financial contributions difficult to track. However, funding for DRR has been quantified. It comprises a fraction of all international aid—less than 0.4 per cent of the $3 trillion spent between 1991 and 2010.[225]

During the past two decades, DRR financing has been "both inadequate and markedly inequitable, with little prioritization across full considerations of risk, need and capacity" and, therefore, has limited results.[226] Of the $363 billion in development aid that went to the top 40 recipients of humanitarian aid between 2000 and 2009, only 1 per cent went to DRR. In 2009, 68 per cent of DRR financing came from humanitarian funds.[227]

Where humanitarian crises are unfolding, or where there is a high risk that they will occur, only a tiny proportion of aid is spent on reducing the risk of future emergencies, and what is being spent is mainly from humanitarian budgets. Even within humanitarian budgets, prevention and preparedness are low priorities, comprising less than 5 per cent of all humanitarian aid in 2011.[228]

Donors differ significantly in their contributions to prevention and preparedness from humanitarian budgets. Only Japan and

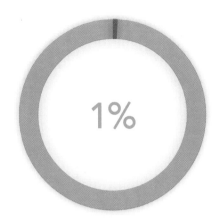

1%

Proportion of development aid to top 40 recipients of humanitarian aid that was spent on DRR (between 2000 and 2009)[229]

Korea spent more than 10 per cent of their humanitarian budgets on disaster prevention and preparedness between 2006 and 2011.[230] In 2011, disaster prevention and preparedness comprised 19 per cent of Australia's bilateral humanitarian assistance, compared with Norway (12 per cent), Japan (10 per cent), EU (8 per cent), US (2 per cent), UK (2 per cent) and France (1 per cent).[231]

The incentives for donors are skewed heavily in favour of funding crisis response. There is less chance of an aid-sceptic public criticising donors for wasting money, and there may be political capital to be gained from high-profile responses, which does not exist for crisis prevention.

However, donors do provide core funding to humanitarian agencies, which can be used to support early action and preparedness activities. This is rarely acknowledged when a crisis occurs, to the frustration of donors.[232]

"A sea change is needed in our approach to international aid financing, one that prioritizes the management of risk… Preparing for current and future risks is a responsibility and a basic requirement for effective humanitarian and development work—it is not optional."

Dare to prepare: taking risk seriously[233]

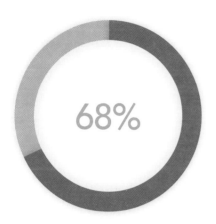

68%

Proportion of spending on DRR in 2009 that came from humanitarian funds[234]

Agencies could decide to increase the proportion of core funding used for crisis-risk management. If these activities are effective, they can reduce costs and provide better value for money in the long term.

Increasing the contribution of development funding

An analysis using an objective measure of crisis risk (the InfoRM risk index)[235] shows that Official Development Assistance (ODA) spending is not correlated with the locations that have the highest risk of humanitarian crises (figure 20).

For example, Central African Republic is third highest in a list of countries ranked for risk, but is the seventy-eighth largest recipient of development aid overall and the seventy-second per capita. When high-risk countries receive large amounts of ODA, it can be volatile. Nigeria and the Republic of Congo saw variations of between 900 and 1,500 per cent in ODA between 2003 and 2006.[236]

Investments in crisis-risk management do not necessarily show immediate results, and it is harder to demonstrate that a crisis was averted than to quantify one when it happens. Countries affected by repeated crisis or with very high crisis risk often have related challenges, such as bad governance and insecurity, which can discourage investment.

A positive trend is the recent prioritization of climate adaptation, which could lead to increased support for crisis-risk management.[237] UNISDR, the World Bank, the OECD and DAC donor Governments have also agreed to establish a means of gauging risk-reducing components within international development assistance, and to provide incentives to increase risk-informed development.[238]

Figure 20

Location of risk and development spending

COUNTRY	InfoRM	ODA	ODA per capita
South Sudan	1	26	46
Somalia	2	25	42
Central Africa Republic	3	78	72
DR of the Congo	4	2	55
Chad	5	59	91
Sudan	6	24	100
Afghanistan	7	1	17
Haiti	8	15	25
Myanmar	9	68	125
Papua New Guinea	10	49	53
Mali	11	22	52
Guinea-Bissau	12	102	65
Ethiopia	13	4	89
Niger	14	44	90
Cote d'Ivoire	15	18	63
Yemen	16	56	104
Cambodia	17	38	78
Nigeria	18	14	115
Madagascar	19	60	105
Bangladesh	20	17	118

The table shows the 20 countries with highest risk according to the preliminary InfoRM risk index for 2014 (source: http://inform.jrc.ec.europa.eu/). Alongside is the position of the country in a ranked list of countries according to net Official Development Assistance and Official Aid received in 2011 and the same indicator per capita (source: World Bank). Development spending shows very low correlation with risk of crises for these data. For example, Central African Republic is third highest in the ranked list for risk, but is the seventy-eighth largest recipient of development aid overall and the seventy-second per capita.

Flexible finance for crisis-risk management

When development funding is flexible, it can react to prevent and mitigate emerging crises. For example, the EU, Australia and Spain can shift a proportion of their development budget in-country to crisis response if necessary.

"Crisis modifiers," which build crisis response into multi-year development grants, have been successful in doing this, but their use is still relatively uncommon. USAID used them in Ethiopia and enabled life-saving interventions to be scaled up during the 2011 drought, but without implementing partners having to submit new proposals. This allowed families to maintain livestock and other assets, with a cost-benefit ratio of 1:40.[239]

> *"We need strategic, long-term partnerships with donors. The impact doesn't come overnight. We need to know that we can rely on their support not only tomorrow. If they want to make a change that lasts, they need to start taking longer breaths."*
>
> Coordinator of local NGO in Lebanon[240]

1:40

Cost to benefit ratio of early interventions to drought in Ethiopia made possible by crisis modifiers in USAID's development programs[243]

Flexible, longer-term humanitarian financing would also enable investments in crisis-risk management. It encourages early action because programmes can scale and adapt more easily. It also helps agencies manage risk more effectively, since programmes such as emergency preparedness and livelihoods support typically require longer commitments.

The Principles of Good Humanitarian Donorship affirm the need for "enhancing the flexibility of" and "introducing longer-term" funding arrangements.[241] Several donors now offer multi-year funding under certain conditions (including Australia, Denmark, Germany, the Netherlands, Norway, Spain, Sweden, Switzerland, the UK, the US and the European Commission).[242] Others should be encouraged to follow.

The Swedish International Development Cooperation Agency made a three-year funding commitment to the Somalia Common Humanitarian Fund. The UK's DFID provided multi-year funding to humanitarian pooled funds in Yemen and Ethiopia. Spain established many multi-year frameworks with various NGOs, which provide pre-allocated funding within days of a proposal being received. Switzerland has a similar funding mechanism through multi-year agreements with partner Governments.

Pooling humanitarian funds to manage risk

Humanitarian pooled funds—including the Central Emergency Response Fund (CERF), country-based common humanitarian funds (CHFs) and emergency response funds (ERFs)—allocated 7.2 per cent of recorded international humanitarian funding in 2012.[244] However, at present they prioritize traditional response activities, with limited investment in prevention and preparedness.[245]

Pooled funds do support early action. For example, CERF allocated $6 million to WFP in Niger in November 2011, based on forecasts of acute food insecurity between June and August 2012.[246]

CERF has discussed the idea of creating an additional preparedness window. However, few interviewees believe this would be a good solution due to fear of fragmenting CERF's role and undermining its effectiveness as a rapid-response fund.

CHFs are only present in some countries, but they could increase their contribution to managing crisis risk. Between 2011 and 2012, the CHFs in Somalia, Sudan and South Sudan allocated $32.8 million to 29 early action projects.[247] In February 2013, the South Sudan CHF allocated $56.5 million for aid and emergency preparedness.[248]

The duration of CHF-financed projects could be increased to support investments in crisis-risk management. In DRC in 2013, donors agreed to fund humanitarian projects for up to 24 months to "address recurrent humanitarian needs that require sustainable interventions of a kind that help[s] build community resilience" and to "reduce the number of short-term emergency actions that respond more to symptoms than to causes."[249] Humanitarian organizations could also build stronger links between CHFs and development-oriented multi donor trust funds.[250]

Avoiding fragmentation

Many funding mechanisms for crisis-risk management exist, but there is still enormous fragmentation. This has led to proposals for dedicated mechanisms to fund risk, but most experts think creating a new fund would be unsuccessful and counterproductive. For example, discussions between ISDR and donors are instead looking to address risk through existing mechanisms, both development and humanitarian.[251]

Basing existing funding on an objective and shared risk assessment would better prioritize flows and promote better coordination among donors. Improved tracking of relevant funding would also help.

"To address recurrent humanitarian needs that require sustainable interventions of a kind that helps build community resilience" and to "reduce the number of short-term emergency actions that respond more to symptoms than to causes."

Rationale for extending the duration of CHF-funded projects in DRC to 2 years[252]

"[Insurance] can help to finance relief, recovery and construction, reduce vulnerability, and provide knowledge and incentives for reducing risk."

IPCC Special Report on Extreme Events[253]

Insurance and sharing risk

Insurance and other risk-transfer mechanisms are good solutions for low-frequency, high-intensity events. They can be market based or share risk between partners.

The Caribbean Catastrophe Risk Insurance Facility (CCRIF)[254] was designed to limit the financial impact of hurricanes and earthquakes by quickly providing funding for Governments. It is a parametric insurance, meaning that a payment is made when a triggering event (hurricane or earthquake) happens, rather than on estimated loss.[255] Since its inception in 2007, CCRIF has paid out $32 million to affected countries, including $4.28 million to Anguilla following Tropical Cyclone Earl in 2010. The value was almost 20 times the annual premium the Government paid for hurricane coverage, determined within 24 hours of the storm, and released within 14 days.[256]

The African Risk Capacity (ARC),[257] led by the African Union, has set up an index-based insurance mechanism for severe drought. By pooling the risk of participating countries, Governments have to invest less money than if they acted individually. Cost-benefit calculations show that $1 spent on early intervention through ARC saves $3.50 in response once a crisis has developed. The economic benefits of helping families before they resort to negative coping mechanisms (such as selling productive assets) can be $1,300 per household.[258] This protection of economic gains, in combination with safety nets and other investments, can promote long-term resilience and reduce reliance on emergency appeals (figure 21).[259]

$32 million

Amount paid to affected countries by the Caribbean Catastrophe Risk Insurance Facility since its inception in 2007[260]

The most vulnerable people usually do not have access to traditional forms of insurance. Micro-insurance is beginning to fill this gap by offering low premiums to people on low incomes. In 2007, 78 million people were covered by micro-insurance; in 2013, 500 million were covered.[261] In many countries, annual growth rates are 10 per cent or higher.[262]

People earning between $1.25 and $4 per day are commercially viable for micro-insurance.[263] Those with a lower income, which includes people affected by humanitarian crises, may still be out of reach. However, they can be insured with support from aid organizations.

In Ethiopia, the Horn of Africa Risk Transfer for Adaption Program allows farmers to pay insurance premiums through labour. It made its first payment following the 2011 drought to more than 1,800 people.[264] In 2012, 12,200 farmers in 45 villages benefited from drought protection, each receiving a share of $300,000 to cover crop losses.[265]

Figure 21

Role of African Risk Capacity (ARC) in increasing resilience to shocks and economic and growth

¹ Resilience Threshold: Limit of national coping capacity. 2 Source: World Bank

³ Current yield in Latin American countries. Source: World Bank. Improvement results from better use of technology in agriculture.

Farmers in the Tigray region of northern Ethiopia face increasingly unpredictable rainfall. "Our season is changing," said Selas Samson Biru. "We don't know when there will be a bad year and when there will be a good year." But he says the insurance will be "helpful during the bad season."²⁶⁶ Another farmer, Medhin Reda, said: "Because of repeated drought, which really affected me, I joined the insurance with the understanding it might solve my problems."²⁶⁷

Insurance and other risk-sharing mechanisms offer tremendous potential. But they come with many challenges, which can be disincentives for private companies. These include educating clients, risk exposure, claims-verification procedures, a lack of formal economy, and insufficient land-tenure procedures or appropriate legislation.²⁶⁸ Supporting more informal community risk-sharing structures may provide an alternative.²⁶⁹ ²⁷⁰

Recommendations

- Donors should base crisis prevention and mitigation funding decisions on risk analysis. They should ensure sufficient funds flow through existing humanitarian and development mechanisms to support the people and countries at highest risk of humanitarian crises.

- Humanitarian and development organizations should ensure that existing funding mechanisms are reviewed and, where appropriate, adjusted to maximize their contribution to managing the risk of humanitarian crises. They should dedicate a higher proportion of their core funding to activities that contribute to managing crisis risk.

- Humanitarian organizations should work with the private sector and other relevant partners to increase the use of risk-transfer mechanisms, such as risk mutualization and micro-insurance.

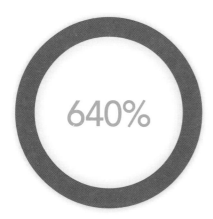

640%

Growth in number of people covered by micro-insurance between 2007 and 2013[274]

Leadership and advocacy

Strong leadership is a prerequisite for the changes to priorities and working methods that a risk-oriented approach requires. For humanitarian organizations, it also entails committed advocacy with Governments and the development sector.

The role of United Nations Resident Coordinator and Humanitarian Coordinator

The United Nations Resident Coordinator (RC) is usually the most senior UN official in a country. Unless there is a dedicated Humanitarian Coordinator (HC), the RC fulfils the role of coordinating international humanitarian assistance.

According to the job description, the RC "encourages and supports national efforts in disaster risk reduction" and "ensures that appropriate linkages are made between relief, recovery, transition and development activities, and promotes prevention strategies in national development plans."[271][272] In practice, however, RCs often have little support and give a low priority to analysing and managing crisis risks. This study found that RC/HCs frequently lacked dedicated capacity and expertise to undertake strategic and coherent humanitarian and development planning.

Some attempts have been made to increase RC capacity in risk management. The IASC, UNDG, UNISDR Common Framework for Capacity Development for Preparedness includes a proposal to develop a pool of disaster risk management advisers to support RCs,[273] but it remains to be seen how this will be implemented. UNDP manages two rosters—the Early Recovery Deployment Mechanism, and the Crisis Prevention and Recovery Consultants Deployment Mechanism—that could support strategic planning.

Additional training for RC/HCs would help. The IASC has implemented several initiatives as part of its Transformative Agenda, including a handbook on emergency preparedness and response. However, dedicated expert capacity, especially at critical parts of the planning cycle, would be more effective in highly vulnerable countries.

Leadership in aid organizations

Most large aid organizations perform humanitarian and development functions. This can cause tensions, especially in conflict settings.[275] [276]

Aid organizations' emergency and development departments are frequently divided, with limited links between their strategies and programmes. When primarily humanitarian organizations take on limited elements of risk management (for example, emergency preparedness), they are often hampered by bureaucratic inertia, divergent operational priorities and contradictory messages.

Strong leadership, as well as clarity on the organization's role in managing risk, can overcome this. But few aid organizations have senior positions dedicated to crisis-risk management. A review of OCHA's preparedness function found a lack of clear responsibility in this area.

Organizational structure, systems and culture need to be adjusted to support crisis-risk management. For example, Oxfam is examining how to better support people's resilience.[277] This includes creating a common organizational narrative on resilience, adjusting tools and structures to support and incentivize comprehensive and integrated work, and reviewing internal language and communication.

Global and regional champions for crisis-risk management

Many of the barriers to better crisis anticipation, prevention and mitigation come down to priority and profile. The involvement of the UN Emergency Relief Coordinator (ERC) and the UNDP Administrator at the earliest stages of the 2011 Sahel crisis raised its profile and saved

"To respond effectively...we need regional Governments working together very effectively, and we need an international community in turn which comes in behind that regional community of actors and dedicates themselves to dealing with the structural problems that are unfolding in the region."

Robert Piper, RHC for the Sahel[278]

lives. National Governments took the lead and more money came in sooner, compared with previous crises.[279]

Donors encouraged humanitarian and development organizations to work together. A Regional Humanitarian Coordinator (RHC) for the Sahel was appointed to support a longer-term cooperative approach.[280] An RHC has also been designated for the Syria crisis.

Informal discussions with donors suggest that high-level advocacy is critical to raising the profile of potential and emerging crises. But the demands of current emergencies limit the time that the ERC can devote to these tasks. Expansion of the RHC role to other regions— with a specific mandate for supporting crisis-risk management—could boost the alignment of humanitarian and development work.

At the international level, a number of champions for crisis-risk management exist, including the Special Representative of the Secretary-General for Disaster Risk Reduction, and the Political Champions for Disaster Resilience, an informal group of senior representatives and political leaders.[281] Their commitment, and that of other leaders, will be critical in increasing the profile of disaster and crisis-risk management in the post-2015 development agenda.

A joint advocacy campaign on crisis prevention

Effective humanitarian action requires effective advocacy among decision makers and the public. Media coverage can strongly influence the profile of and response to crises. Large humanitarian crises, especially sudden-onset disasters such as Haiti in 2010 and the Philippines in 2013, trigger international attention and support.

Preventing crises rarely elicits a similar response, but there have been some successes, especially on the back of significant disasters. In Turkey, for example, Turkcell conducted an SMS fundraising campaign following the Van earthquake in 2011 to ensure education would not be disrupted in future disasters. It raised TRY5 million ($2.3 million) for earthquake-proof dormitories, and housing and education scholarships.[282]

Improving advocacy is crucial. In 2012, OCHA and UNDP launched the "Act Now, Save Later" disaster-preparedness campaign,[283] but there is a lack of targeted, high-level campaigns on prevention. Nonetheless, road-safety improvements in many countries show that the right combination of policies, legislation and advocacy can achieve significant results.[284] Road-safety measures in the EU decreased fatalities by half between 1991 and 2009.[285]

The disparate institutional makeup of humanitarian relief, DRR and development organizations make this a complex process. However, a well-resourced joint advocacy campaign for crisis prevention, including donors, could increase its priority. The post-2015 development agenda and the World

Humanitarian Summit in 2016 offer the best opportunities for such a campaign in many years.

Recommendations

- Humanitarian organizations should appoint senior leaders with responsibility for crisis-risk management, as well as RHCs to align their risk-management work with Governments, international organizations and donors. RHCs can be advocates of preparedness and early action.

- Humanitarian and development organizations should increase the capacity of the RC/HC for risk analysis and strategic planning, for example through an expert roster system.

- Humanitarian organizations should launch a joint, global advocacy campaign on preventing humanitarian crises, focused on the post-2015 development agenda and the outcomes of the World Humanitarian Summit in 2016. This should include the use of high-level 'global champions'.

$2.3 million

Amount raised by Turkcell campaign after the Van earthquake to ensure education would not be disrupted in future disasters[286]

A global dialogue

Palestinian children fly kites to show their solidarity with the Japanese people during an event marking the anniversary of the Great East Japan Earthquake of 2011. Japan is one of the world's leading countries when it comes to disaster risk reduction and preparedness. This report calls for a global dialogue on preventing future humanitarian crises.

CHAPTER 4
Conclusions and recommendations

Rising needs, new risks, old problems

The number of people facing humanitarian crises is rising, and the international humanitarian system cannot keep up. Climate change, food-price volatility and other emerging threats have **increased the risk and complexity of crises,** making them bigger, longer and more difficult to deal with. Chronic, recurring crises have eroded people's ability to cope, rendering them increasingly vulnerable to future calamities. Humanitarian organizations are being asked **to do more, and at greater cost, than ever before.** Development programming is often not targeted at the people most at risk of humanitarian crises, or sufficiently flexible to respond to changing risks and potential crises.

But there is a way forward. For the humanitarian system to adapt to a world of rising challenges, it needs to **shift from crisis response to crisis-risk management.** This means developing a shared, broader understanding of the risks that lead to humanitarian crises, and **working across institutional divides** to prioritize and manage them comprehensively.

All crises are different. Sudden disasters resulting from earthquakes, floods and storms, the creeping effects of drought and the pressure of increasing food prices on already destitute people all require different approaches to risk management. Conflict poses unique challenges. Nevertheless, the concept of crisis-risk management, **going beyond simple response,** is universal.

Managing the risk of humanitarian crises

For the humanitarian sector, it means programming to prepare for and react early to warning signs, and delivering aid that helps people build a sustainable future. It requires predictable and flexible financing, which adequately prioritizes crisis prevention and mitigation. It also needs leadership committed to strengthening links with Governments and development organizations.

To do this effectively, humanitarian and development groups need to build greater national and local capacity to manage risk. This includes emergency preparedness and community early warning systems. They must move to a more service-oriented approach—providing assistance to Governments outside of crises, and working through Government structures where possible.

Governments also need to manage the risk of crises as a fundamental component of economic and social development. Where Governments take the lead, links between humanitarian and development work are increased, and their impact multiplied. Where joint risk-management initiatives exist, they need to be scaled up and more comprehensively address risk—not just one element or activity. When agencies participate in such initiatives, they need to devote sufficient resources to make them a success. Donors can provide incentives for collaboration.

Risk analysis can support crisis anticipation and prevention, as well as the prioritization of resources. It can also help identify longer-term solutions to crises. But analysis is not enough. Early warning systems must be matched by mechanisms to take action. Consensus should be reached on triggers for early action, such as detailed assessments and the development of response options. National and local processes should be developed to analyse and monitor risk, share information and reach consensus.

Effective risk management needs to work in the short, medium and longer term. This means addressing people's immediate needs, helping them recover and addressing their underlying problems.

Traditionally, humanitarian planning has focused on the short term and development on the long term. Better alignment between the two is critical. There is also a gap in medium-term activities (one to five years), such as emergency preparedness, which needs to be addressed.

Programming faces similar challenges. Humanitarian programming is overwhelmingly focused on short-term response, while development programming is often not well targeted at the people and places most vulnerable to humanitarian crises. There remains a fundamental deficit in medium-term programming (for example, emergency preparedness, early action, livelihood support and early recovery) to help people prepare for, cope with and recover from crises, and become more resilient.

For programming to help people prevent and manage crises, it needs a comprehensive approach to risk. A holistic approach to drought management, for example, can concurrently meet immediate needs with material assistance or cash, tackle underlying causes through better land management and manage longer-term risk through insurance.

Significant additional resources are needed to make this work. Prevention-and-preparedness programmes currently comprise a fraction of all international aid and tend to be poorly targeted, failing the most vulnerable. Development funding needs to make a larger contribution to crisis prevention. This can be done by integrating crisis prevention and risk reduction into development plans, and making those plans flexible enough to adapt to emerging crises.

Humanitarian planning and funding mechanisms can also support crisis-risk management. Multi-year planning and funding can improve links to development plans; pooled funds offer opportunities to strengthen crisis-risk management. The main challenge, however, is to improve programming. When effective programmes exist, funding will follow.

Making these changes to the aid system will require strong leadership and sustained public advocacy on a national and international stage. Senior leaders need to champion risk management in the run up to 2015 and beyond.

On the ground, RCs should improve links between humanitarian and development work, and increase their risk-analysis and strategic-planning capacity. Appointing RHCs can promote a more risk-focused approach.

A global dialogue on managing crisis risk

The shift from cure to prevention is a political challenge at multiple levels. It has implications for politics in the affected countries, between and within aid agencies and in donor countries. It will not be easy.

But this challenge has been overcome countless times, in many walks of life, as people have built common systems to address future problems. If road-safety experts can convince people to wear seatbelts, humanitarian organizations and others can learn to manage risk.

The implementation of a new global development framework after 2015, and the World Humanitarian Summit in 2016, offers a once-in-a-generation opportunity to change tack and put risk at the core of the aid system—to shift from seeing crises not as external events, but as the consequence of our ability to manage risk.

This requires a global discussion on preventing humanitarian crises, which includes Governments, donors, international organizations, civil society and the private sector. This report is intended to start and support that discussion.

Recommendations

This report presents a humanitarian perspective on a long-standing problem: how to prevent suffering in future crises. Its recommendations are not a perfect answer and not the only solutions. However, if adapted to different contexts they would help make the current aid system more effective.

Make preventing future humanitarian crises a priority

- Governments should prioritize crisis-risk management in order to prevent and mitigate future humanitarian crises. They should address the underlying drivers of risk through all Government functions; provide livelihood options, basic services and social protection for the most vulnerable people; and set up systems for crisis anticipation, preparedness and response.

- Humanitarian organizations should increase and formalize their role in managing the risk of crises, work more closely with Governments to build national and local capacity, and provide aid that meets immediate needs and addresses future risk.

- Governments should ensure that development aid targets the people and countries most at risk from humanitarian crises. Crisis risk management should be fully integrated into national development plans, bilateral framework agreements and specifically included in the post-2015 development agenda.

- Humanitarian organizations should launch a joint, global advocacy campaign on preventing humanitarian crises, focused on the post-2015 development agenda and the outcomes of the World Humanitarian Summit in 2016. This should include the use of high-level 'global champions.'

Create new partnerships and incentives

- Humanitarian and development organizations should support existing and develop new joint initiatives that contribute to crisis anticipation, prevention, mitigation and recovery. They should also make long-term commitments of resources to those initiatives. Multi-mandated organizations and donors should strengthen links between their humanitarian and development teams, for example through joint planning cells.

- Where one does not exist, Governments and partners should establish a national coordination forum to jointly analyse and address risks, monitor and share early warning information, and develop triggers for action. Humanitarian organizations may need to establish similar, independent processes in conflict situations.

- Humanitarian organizations should appoint senior leaders with responsibility for crisis-risk management, as well as Regional HCs to align their risk-management work with Governments, international organizations and donors. RHCs can be advocates of preparedness and early action.

Work differently and systematically address risk

- Humanitarian and development organizations and donors should base their planning on a common analysis of risk and align their planning cycles where possible. They should support tools and processes to jointly analyse crisis risk, such as the InfoRM initiative.

- Humanitarian and development organizations should increase the capacity of the RC/HC for risk analysis and strategic planning, for example through an expert roster system.

- Humanitarian organizations should increase the length of their planning cycle to three years in protracted crises. They should increase their use of programmatic approaches–including preparedness, livelihood support and cash-transfer programming–to help communities manage the risk of crises.

Dedicate resources today to save lives tomorrow

- Donors should base crisis prevention and mitigation funding decisions on risk analysis. They should ensure sufficient funds flow through existing humanitarian and development mechanisms to support the people and countries at highest risk of humanitarian crises.

- Humanitarian and development organizations should ensure that existing funding mechanisms are reviewed and, where appropriate, adjusted to maximize their contribution to managing the risk of humanitarian crises. They should dedicate a higher proportion of their core funding to activities that contribute to managing crisis risk.

- Humanitarian organizations should work with the private sector and other relevant partners to increase the use of risk-transfer mechanisms, such as risk mutualization and micro-insurance.

REFERENCES

[1] United Nations Office for the Coordination of Humanitarian Affairs (2014). Overview of Global Humanitarian Response 2014. Available from: www.docs.unocha.org/sites/dms/CAP/Overview_of_Global_Humanitarian_ Response_2014.pdf

[2] IRIN. Manbahadur Tamang – Farmer, Nepal. Available from: www.irinnews.org/in-depth/98329/98/

[3] IRIN. Manbahadur Tamang – Farmer, Nepal. Available from: www.irinnews.org/in-depth/98329/98/

[4] United Nations Office for the Coordination of Humanitarian Affairs (2013). World Humanitarian Data and Trends 2013. Available from: docs.unocha.org/sites/dms/Documents/WHDT_2013%20WEB.pdf

[5] United Nations Office for the Coordination of Humanitarian Affairs (2013). World Humanitarian Data and Trends 2013. Available from: docs.unocha.org/sites/dms/Documents/WHDT_2013%20WEB.pdf

[6] PovcalNet: the on-line tool for poverty measurement developed by the Development Research Group of the World Bank. Available from: iresearch.worldbank.org/PovcalNet/

[7] Food and Agriculture Organization of the United Nations (2012). The State of Food Insecurity in the World. Available from: www.fao.org/docrep/016/i2845e/i2845e00.pdf

[8] Chandy, L., Gertz, G. (2011). Poverty in Numbers: The Changing State of Global Poverty from 2005 to 2015. Policy Brief 2011-01. Brookings Institution. Available from: www.brookings.edu/~/media/research/files/papers/2011/1/ global%20poverty%20chandy/01_global_poverty_chandy.pdf

[9] United Nations Office for the Coordination of Humanitarian Affairs (2013). Overview of Global Humanitarian Response 2013 at Mid-Year. Available from: docs.unocha.org/sites/dms/CAP/MYR_2013_Overview_of_GHA.pdf

[10] IRIN. SAHEL: Region is "ground zero" for climate change – Egeland. Available from: www.irinnews.org/ report/78515/sahel-region-is-ground-zero-for-climate-change-egeland

[11] Hillier, D. Nightingale, K. (2013). How Disasters Disrupt Development: Recommendations for the Post-2015 Development Framework. Oxfam International. Available from: reliefweb.int/sites/reliefweb.int/files/resources/ib- disasters-disrupt-development-post2015-111213-en.pdf

[12] Global Humanitarian Assistance (2013). Global Humanitarian Assistance Report 2013. Available from: www. globalhumanitarianassistance.org/wp-content/uploads/2013/07/GHA-Report-20131.pdf

[13] Kellett, J. & Caravani, A. (2013). Financing Disaster Risk Reduction. A 20 year story of international aid. Overseas Development Institute & Global Facility for Disaster Reduction and Recovery. Available from: www.odi.org.uk/sites/ odi.org.uk/files/odi-assets/publications-opinion-files/8574.pdf

[14] International Federation of Red Cross and Red Crescent Societies. (2008). Early Warning > Early Action. Available from: www.ifrc.org/Global/Publications/disasters/ew-ea-2008.pdf

[15] Kellett, J. & Caravani, A. (2013). Financing Disaster Risk Reduction. A 20 year story of international aid. Overseas Development Institute & Global Facility for Disaster Reduction and Recovery. Available from: www.odi.org.uk/sites/ odi.org.uk/files/odi-assets/publications-opinion-files/8574.pdf

[16] Kellet, J. & Caravani, A. (2013). Financing Disaster Risk Reduction. A 20 year story of international aid. Overseas Development Institute & Global Facility for Disaster Reduction and Recovery. Available from: www.odi.org.uk/sites/ odi.org.uk/files/odi-assets/publications-opinion-files/8574.pdf

[17] Global Humanitarian Assistance (2013). Global Humanitarian Assistance Report 2013. Available from: www.globalhumanitarianassistance.org/wp-content/uploads/2013/07/GHA-Report-20131.pdf

[18] Southern African Regional Inter-agency Standing Committee (RIASCO) (2014). Humanitarian Trends in Southern Africa: Challenges and Opportunities. Available from: reliefweb.int/report/malawi/humanitarian-trends-southern-africa-challenges-and-opportunities

[19] United Nations (2013). United Nations Plan of Action on Disaster Risk Reduction for Resilience. Available at: www.preventionweb.net/files/33703_actionplanweb14.06cs[1].pdf

[20] United Nations Office for the Coordination of Humanitarian Affairs (2013). World Humanitarian Data and Trends 2013. Available from: docs.unocha.org/sites/dms/Documents/WHDT_2013%20WEB.pdf

[21] United Nations High Commissioner for Refugees (2012). UNHCR Global Trends 2012: Displacement, The New 21st Century Challenge. Available from: www.unhcr.org/globaltrendsjune2013/UNHCR%20GLOBAL%20TRENDS%202012_V08_web.pdf

[22] Guha-Sapir, D., Hoyois, P. & Below, R. (2012). "Annual Disaster Statistical Review 2012: The numbers and trends". Centre for Research on the Epidemiology of Disasters (CRED), Institute of Health and Society (IRSS), Université catholique de Louvain. Available from: cred.be/sites/default/files/ADSR_2012.pdf

[23] United Nations (2011). Revealing Risk, Redefining Development: Global Assessment Report on Disaster Risk Reduction. Available from: www.preventionweb.net/english/hyogo/gar/2011/en/home/download.html

[24] World Bank & Global Facility for Disaster Reduction and Recovery (2013). Building Resilience: Integrating Climate and Disaster Risk into Development. Available from: www-wds.worldbank.org/external/default/WDSContentServer/WDSP/IB/2013/11/14/000456286_20131114153130/Rendered/PDF/826480WP0v10Bu0130Box379862000UO090.pdf

[25] United Nations (2011). Revealing Risk, Redefining Development: Global Assessment Report on Disaster Risk Reduction. Available from: www.preventionweb.net/english/hyogo/gar/2011/en/home/download.html

[26] World Meteorological Organization (2010). Bulletin. Vol. 59 (2) – 2010. Available from www.wmo.int/pages/publications/bulletin_en/archive/59_2_en/documents/bulletin_en.pdf

[27] Banyaneer (2013). "What Exactly is Resilience?" In brief, September 2013, No. 1. Available from: banyaneer.com/wp-content/uploads/2013/08/Resilience.pdf

[28] UN News Centre. Typhoon Haiyan wake-up call to speed up Climate Control Efforts – Ban. Available from: www.un.org/apps/news//story.asp?NewsID=46520&Cr=haiyan&Cr1=

[29] Food and Agriculture Organization of the United Nations, (2008) Climate Change and Food Security: A Framework Document. Available from: www.fao.org/forestry/15538-079b31d45081fe9c3dbc6ff34de4807e4.pdf

[30] World Bank (2012) Turn Down the Heat: Why a 4C Warmer World Must be Avoided. Available from: climatechange.worldbank.org/sites/default/files/Turn_Down_the_heat_Why_a_4_degree_centrigrade_warmer_world_must_be_avoided.pdf

[31] Bobenrieth, E. S. & Wright, B. D. (2009) The Food price crisis of 2007/2008: Evidence and Implications. Available from: www.fao.org/fileadmin/templates/est/meetings/joint_igg_grains/Panel_Discussion_paper_2_English_only.pdf

[32] Gros, A., Gard-Murray, A., Bar-Yam, Y. (2012). Conflict in Yemen: From Ethnic Fighting to Food Riots. New England Complex Systems Institute. Available from: necsi.edu/research/social/yemen/Yemen_Conflict.pdf

[33] United Nations (2013). Mid-Year Review of the Humanitarian Response Plan for Yemen 2013. Available from: www.unocha.org/cap/appeals/mid-year-review-humanitarian-response-plan-yemen-2013

[34] Lagi, M., Bertrand, K. & Bar-Yam, Y. (2011). The Food Crisis and Political Instability in North Africa and the Middle East. Available from: necsi.edu/research/social/food_crises.pdf

[35] British Red Cross (2012). Learning from the City. Available from: reliefweb.int/sites/reliefweb.int/files/resources/Learning%20from%20the%20City%20%282012%29_0.pdf

[36] IPCC (2012). Summary for Policymakers. Managing the Risks of Extreme Events and Disasters to Advance Climate Change Adaptation. Available from: ipcc-wg2.gov/SREX/images/uploads/SREX-SPMbrochure_FINAL.pdf

[37] United Nations Environment Programme (2011). Livelihood Security Climate Change, Migration and Conflict in the Sahel. Available from: postconflict.unep.ch/publications/UNEP_Sahel_EN.pdf

[38] Bobenrieth, E. S. & Wright, B. D. (2009) The Food price crisis of 2007/2008: Evidence and Implications. Available from: www.fao.org/fileadmin/templates/est/meetings/joint_igg_grains/Panel_Discussion_paper_2_English_only.pdf

[39] United Nations Office for the Coordination of Humanitarian Affairs (2013). World Humanitarian Data and Trends 2013. Available from: docs.unocha.org/sites/dms/Documents/WHDT_2013%20WEB.pdf

[40] Aning, K. & Atta-Asamoah, A. (2011) Demography, Environment and Conflict in East Africa. KAIPTC Occasional Paper N.34 Available from: dspace.cigilibrary.org/jspui/bitstream/123456789/31687/1/Occasional-Paper-34-Aning-and-Asamoah.pdf?1

[41] Population Action International (2012). "Why Population Matters to Poverty Reduction". Available from: populationaction.org/policy-briefs/why-population-matters-to-poverty-reduction/

[42] Cincotta, R., Englemen, R., Anastasion, D. (2003). "The Security Demographic: Population and Civil Conflict After the Cold War". Available from: populationaction.org/reports/the-security-demographic-population-and-civil-conflict-after-the-cold-war/

[43] Food and Agriculture Organization of the United Nations (2012). The State of Food Insecurity in the World. Available from: www.fao.org/docrep/016/i2845e/i2845e00.pdf

[44] IEA (2013) World Energy Outlook 2013: Executive Summary. Available from: www.iea.org/publications/freepublications/publication/WEO2013_Executive_Summary_English.pdf

[45] IPCC (2013) Final Draft: Underlying Scientific-Technical Assessment. Working Group I Contribution to the IPCC Fifth Assessment Report Climate Change 2013: Physical Science Basis. Available from: www.climatechange2013.org/images/uploads/WGIAR5_WGI-12Doc2b_FinalDraft_All.pdf

[46] United Nations (2013) World Population Prospects: The 2012 Revision. Available from: esa.un.org/unpd/wpp/Documentation/pdf/WPP2012_HIGHLIGHTS.pdf

[47] United Nations (2009) Water in a Changing World. The UN World Water Development Report. Available from: www.unesco.org/new/fileadmin/MULTIMEDIA/HQ/SC/pdf/WWDR3_Facts_and_Figures.pdf

[48] UNWATER. Statistics. Available from: www.unwater.org/statistics.html

[49] OECD (2008) OECD Environmental Outlook to 2030. Available from: www.oecd.org/environment/indicators-modelling-outlooks/40200582.pdf

[50] Ravallion, M. & Chen, S. (2012). More Relatively-Poor People in a Less Absolutely-Poor World. Policy Research Working Paper 6114. Available from: http://www-wds.worldbank.org/servlet/WDSContentServer/WDSP/IB/2012/07/02/000158349_20120702111420/Rendered/PDF/WPS6114.pdf

[51] Brown, S., Nicholls, R., Vafeidis, A., Hinkel, J. and Watkiss, P. (2011) The Impacts and Economic Costs of Sea-Level Rise in Europe and the Costs and Benefits of Adaptation. Summary of Results from the EC RTD ClimateCost Project. In Watkiss, P (Editor), 2011. The ClimateCost Project. Final Report. Volume 1: Europe. Available from: www.climatecost.cc/images/Policy_brief_2_Coastal_10_lowres.pdf

[52] WHO / UNICEF Joint Monitoring Programme (JMP) for Water Supply and Sanitation. Available at: www.wssinfo.org/

[53] PovcalNet: the on-line tool for poverty measurement developed by the Development Research Group of the World Bank. Available from: iresearch.worldbank.org/PovcalNet/

[54] Humanitarian Coalition. What is a humanitarian crisis? Available from: http://humanitariancoalition.ca/info-portal/factsheets/what-is-a-humanitarian-crisis

[55] United Nations International Strategy for Disaster Reduction (2007). "Terminology". Available from: www.unisdr.org/we/inform/terminology

[56] IPCC (2012). "Managing the Risks of Extreme Events and Disasters to Advance Climate Change Adaptation. A Special Report of Working Groups I and II of the Intergovernmental Panel on Climate Change". Cambridge University Press, Cambridge, UK and New York, NY, USA.

[57] IPCC (2012). "Managing the Risks of Extreme Events and Disasters to Advance Climate Change Adaptation. A Special Report of Working Groups I and II of the Intergovernmental Panel on Climate Change". Cambridge University Press, Cambridge, UK and New York, NY, USA.

[58] United Nations International Strategy for Disaster Reduction (2013). Philippines plea: 'stop this climate madness'. Available from: www.unisdr.org/archive/35439

[59] IFR. What is vulnerability? Available from: www.unisdr.org/we/inform/terminology

[60] United Nations International Strategy for Disaster Reduction (2007). "Terminology". Available from: www.unisdr.org/we/inform/terminology

[61] World Bank (2013). World Development Report 2014: Risk and Opportunity. Available from: siteresources.worldbank.org/EXTNWDR2013/Resources/8258024-1352909193861/8936935-1356011448215/8986901-1380046989056/WDR-2014_Complete_Report.pdf

[62] OECD (2011). Managing Risks in Fragile and Transitional Contexts: The Price of Success? Available from: www.oecd.org/dac/incaf/48634348.pdf

[63] US NAVY. Joint Typhoon Warning Center. Available at: www.usno.navy.mil/JTWC/

[64] Oxfam America (2009). Weather Insurance Offers Ethiopian Farmers Hope—Despite Drought. Available from: www.oxfamamerica.org/articles/weather-insurance-offers-ethiopian-farmers-hope-despite-drought

[65] World Economic Forum (2013). "Global Risks 2013". Available from: www3.weforum.org/docs/WEF_GlobalRisks_Report_2013.pdf

[66] Pew Research Center (2013). Despite Challenges, Africans Are Optimistic about the Future Available from: www.pewglobal.org/files/2013/11/Pew-Research-Center-Global-Attitudes-Africa-Release-FINAL-October-8-20132.pdf

[67] Food and Agriculture Organization of the United Nations (2009). Responding to the food crisis: synthesis of medium-term measures proposed in inter-agency assessments. Available from : www.fao.org/fileadmin/user_upload/ISFP/SR_Web.pdf

[68] United Nations Office for the Coordination of Humanitarian Affairs (2008). Consolidated Appeal 2008. Available from: docs.unocha.org/sites/dms/CAP/Flash_2008_Tajikistan.pdf

[69] Akramov, K. & Shreedhar, G. (2012) Economic Development, External Shocks, and Food Security in Tajikistan. IFPRI Discussion Paper 01163. Available from: www.ifpri.org/sites/default/files/publications/ifpridp01163.pdf

[70] See www.unicef.org/tajikistan/reallives_8270.html

[71] Information and findings, kindly provided by the Southern Africa Regional Inter-Agency Standing Committee (RIASCO), Ignacio León-Garcia (Head of the OCHA Regional Office for Southern Africa) and Dr. Ailsa Holloway (Stellenbosch University), from the report "Humanitarian Trends in Southern Africa: Challenges and Opportunities".

[72] See ec.europa.eu/echo/civil_protection/civil/indo_2006.htm

[73] IFRC (2009). West Java Earthquake: Information Bulletin. Available from: www.ifrc.org/docs/appeals/rpts09/ideq07090902.pdf

[74] Yakkum Emergency Unit (2009) Indonesia: West Sumatra Earthquake 2009
Available from: reliefweb.int/report/indonesia/indonesia-west-sumatra-earthquake-2009

[75] IFRC (2009). Indonesia: West Sumatra Earthquakes. Emergency Appeal Final Report. Available from: www.ifrc.org/docs/appeals/09/MDRID004fr.pdf

[76] ECHO (2013). Indonesia: Fact Sheet. Available from: ec.europa.eu/echo/files/aid/countries/factsheets/indonesia_en.pdf

[77] United Nations DESA (2013) World Population Prospects: The 2012 Revision Highlights and Advance Tables.
Available from: esa.un.org/unpd/wpp/Documentation/pdf/WPP2012_HIGHLIGHTS.pdf

[78] Engvall, J. (2011). "Flirting with State Failure". Available from: www.isdp.eu/publications/index.php?option=com_jombib&task=showbib&id=5990

[79] ILO (2010) Migrant Remittances to Tajikistan. Available from: www.ilo.org/public/english/region/eurpro/moscow/info/publ/tajik_migr_remit_en.pdf

[80] IASC (2012) Plan de réponse face à la crise alimentaire et nutritionnelle au Sahel. Available from : http://reliefweb.int/report/burkina-faso/document-strat%C3%A9gique-2012-version-2-plan-de-r%C3%A9ponse-face-%C3%A0-la-crise-alimentaire

[81] United Nations Office for the Coordination of Humanitarian Affairs (2013). Burkina Faso Consolidated Appeal Mid-Year Review 2013. Available from: reliefweb.int/sites/reliefweb.int/files/resources/MYR_2013_Burkina_Faso.pdf

[82] Southern African Regional Inter-agency Standing Committee (RIASCO) (2014). Humanitarian Trends in Southern Africa: Challenges and Opportunities. Available from: www.reliefweb.int/report/malawi/humanitarian-trends-southern-africa-challenges-and-opportunities

[83] Hallegatte, S. (2012) A Cost Effective Solution to Reduce Disaster Losses in Developing Countries: Hydro-Meteorological Services, Early Warning, and Evacuation. Policy Research Working Paper 6058. Available from: www-wds.worldbank.org/external/default/WDSContentServer/WDSP/IB/2012/05/04/000158349_20120504094326/Rendered/PDF/WPS6058.pdf

[84] Khan, F., Mustafa, D., D., Kull and The Risk to Resilience Study Team, (2008): Evaluating the Costs and Benefits of Disaster Risk Reduction under Changing Climatic Conditions: A Pakistan Case Study, From Risk to Resilience Working Paper No. 7. Available from: risk.earthmind.net/files/ProVention-2008-Evaluating-Costs-Benefits-Pakistan-Case-Study.pdf

[85] Barnett, M. & Ramalingan, B. (2010). The Humanitarian's Dilemma: collective action or inaction in international relief? Available from: www.odi.org.uk/sites/odi.org.uk/files/odi-assets/publications-opinion-files/5840.pdf

[86] Moyo, D. (2009). Dead Aid: Why Aid is Not Working and How There is a Better Way for Africa. Farrar, Straus and Giroux.

[87] Polman, L. (2011). The Crisis Caravan. Picador.

[88] Cabot Vention, C., Fitzgibbon, C., Shitarek, T. et al. (2012). The Economics of Early Response and Disaster Resilience: Lessons from Kenya and Ethiopia. June. Available from: www.gov.uk/government/uploads/system/uploads/attachment_data/file/67330/Econ-Ear-Rec-Res-Full-Report_20.pdf

[89] See www.ifrc.org/docs/news/08/08040901/

[90] Hallegatte, S. (2012) A Cost Effective Solution to Reduce Disaster Losses in Developing Countries: Hydro-Meteorological Services, Early Warning, and Evacuation. Policy Research Working Paper 6058. Available from: www-wds.worldbank.org/external/default/WDSContentServer/WDSP/IB/2012/05/04/000158349_20120504094326/Rendered/PDF/WPS6058.pdf

[91] Khan, F., Mustafa, D., D., Kull and The Risk to Resilience Study Team, (2008): Evaluating the Costs and Benefits of Disaster Risk Reduction under Changing Climatic Conditions: A Pakistan Case Study, From Risk to Resilience. Working Paper No. 7. Available from: http://risk.earthmind.net/files/ProVention-2008-Evaluating-Costs-Benefits-Pakistan-Case-Study.pdf

[92] United Nations Office for the Coordination of Humanitarian Affairs (2013) Humanitarianism in the Network Age. Available from: docs.unocha.org/sites/dms/Documents/WEB%20Humanitarianism%20in%20the%20Network%20Age%20vF%20single.pdf

[93] Pew Research Center (2013) Climate Change and Financial Instability Seen as Top Global Threats. Available from: www.pewglobal.org/files/2013/06/Pew-Research-Center-Global-Attitudes-Project-Global-Threats-Report-FINAL-June-24-20131.pdf

[94] Food and Agriculture Organization of the United Nations (2003). Participatory Development: Guidelines on Beneficiary Participation in Agricultural and Rural Development. Available from: ftp://ftp.fao.org/docrep/fao/007/AD817E/AD817E00.pdf

[95] World Bank (2013). World Development Report 2014: Risk and Opportunity. Available from: siteresources.worldbank.org/EXTNWDR2013/Resources/8258024-1352909193861/8936935-1356011448215/8986901-1380046989056/WDR-2014_Complete_Report.pdf

[96] IRIN. Linking Early Warning to Early Action in The Sahel. Available from: www.irinnews.org/report/98244/linking-early-warning-to-early-action-in-the-sahel

[97] Foresight Reducing Risks of Future Disasters: Priorities for Decision Makers (2012). Final Project Report.The Government Office for Science, London. Available from: www.bis.gov.uk/assets/foresight/docs/reducing-risk-management/12-1289-reducing-risks-of-future-disasters-report.pdf

[98] Foresight (2012). Reducing Risks of Future Disasters: Priorities for Decision Makers. Available from: www.bis.gov.uk/assets/foresight/docs/reducing-risk-management/12-1289-reducing-risks-of-future-disasters-report.pdf

[99] The Economist. Bonds Pay Out When Catastrophe Strikes are Rising Popularity Perilous Paper. Available from: www.economist.com/news/finance-and-economics/21587229-bonds-pay-out-when-catastrophe-strikes-are-rising-popularity-perilous-paper

[100] Mitchell, T. & Harris, K. (2012). Resilience: A Risk Management Approach. Background Note. ODI. Available from: www.odi.org.uk/sites/odi.org.uk/files/odi-assets/publications-opinion-files/7552.pdf

[101] Mitchell, T. & Harris, K. (2012). Resilience: A Risk Management Approach. Background Note. ODI. Available from: www.odi.org.uk/sites/odi.org.uk/files/odi-assets/publications-opinion-files/7552.pdf

[102] United Nations. The Universal Declaration of Human Rights. Available from: www.un.org/en/documents/udhr/

[103] United Nations (2005). Hyogo Framework for Action 2005-2015. Available from: www.unisdr.org/files/1037_hyogoframeworkforactionenglish.pdf

[104] Valencia-Ospina, E. (2013). Sixth report on the protection of persons in the event of disasters, by, Special Rapporteur. United Nations A/CN.4/662 General Assembly Distr.: General. Available from: www.un.org/law/ilc/

[105] Province of British Colombia Risk Management Branch and Government Security Office (2012). Risk Management Guideline for the British Colombia Public Sector. Available from: www.fin.gov.bc.ca/pt/rmb/ref/RMB_ERM_Guideline.pdf

[106] The Paris Declaration on Aid Effectiveness (2005). Available from: www.oecd.org/redirect/dataoecd/11/41/34428351.pdf

[107] International Red Cross and Red Crescent Movement (1995) The Code of Conduct for the International Red Cross and Red Crescent Movement and NGOs in Disaster Relief. Available from: www.ifrc.org/Docs/idrl/I259EN.pdf

[108] Principles and Good Practice of Humanitarian Donorship. Available from: Good Available from: www.goodhumanitariandonorship.org/Libraries/Ireland_Doc_Manager/EN-23-Principles-and-Good-Practice-of-Humanitarian-Donorship.sflb.ashx

[109] Of which 63% have more than 11 years of experience in the humanitarian and/or development field.

[110] United Nations Office for the Coordination of Humanitarian Affairs (2013) Exchange of Practices and Lessons Learnt on Resilience Building in the Horn of Africa and the Sahel Regions. Workshop Report. Available from: urd.org/IMG/pdf/Horn_Sahel_Resilience_Workshop_Report_-_final.pdf

[111] United Nations Office for the Coordination of Humanitarian Affairs (2013) Humanitarianism in the Network Age. Available from: docs.unocha.org/sites/dms/Documents/WEB%20Humanitarianism%20in%20the%20Network%20Age%20vF%20single.pdf

[112] Harvard Humanitarian Initiative (2011). Disaster Relief 2.0: The Future of Information Sharing in Humanitarian Emergencies Available from: www.unfoundation.org/assets/pdf/disaster-relief-20-report.pdf

[113] Bailey, R. (2013). Managing Famine Risk: Linking Early Warning to Early Action. Chatham House. Available from: www.chathamhouse.org/sites/default/files/public/Research/Energy,%20Environment%20and%20Development/0413r_earlywarnings.pdf

[114] Slim, H. (2012). IASC Real-Time Evaluation of the Humanitarian Response to the Horn of Africa Drought Crisis in Somalia, Ethiopia and Kenya. Available from: reliefweb.int/sites/reliefweb.int/files/resources/RTE_HoA_SynthesisReport_FINAL.pdf

[115] IRIN. Linking Early Warning to Early Action in The Sahel. Available from: www.irinnews.org/report/98244/linking-early-warning-to-early-action-in-the-sahel

[116] Development Initiatives (2013). Global Humanitarian Assistance Report 2013. Available from: www.globalhumanitarianassistance.org/

[117] Development Initiatives (2013). Global Humanitarian Assistance Report 2013. Available from: www.globalhumanitarianassistance.org/

[118] DARA (2011). The Humanitarian Response Index 2011. Addressing the Gender Challenge. Available from: daraint.org/wp-content/uploads/2012/03/HRI_2011_Complete_Report.pdf

[119] Bailey, R. (2013). Managing Famine Risk: Linking Early Warning to Early Action. Chatham House. Available from: www.chathamhouse.org/sites/default/files/public/Research/Energy,%20Environment%20and%20Development/0413r_earlywarnings.pdf

[120] Bailey, R. (2013). Managing Famine Risk: Linking Early Warning to Early Action. Chatham House. Available from: www.chathamhouse.org/sites/default/files/public/Research/Energy,%20Environment%20and%20Development/0413r_earlywarnings.pdf.

[121] DARA (2011). The Humanitarian Response Index 2011: Addressing the Gender Challenge. Available from: daraint.org/wp-content/uploads/2012/03/HRI_2011_Complete_Report.pdf

[122] The Guardian. Ten Ways 10 ways to make humanitarian efforts complement development. Available from: www.theguardian.com/global-development-professionals-network/2013/oct/09/humanitarian-response-development-crises-best-bits

[123] High Level Task Force on the Global Food Crisis (2010). Updated Comprehensive Framework for Action. Available from: un-foodsecurity.org/sites/default/files/UCFA_English.pdf

[124] Lusthaus, C. & McLean, D. (2013). Independent External Evaluation of the HLTF Coordination Team. Available from: un-foodsecurity.org/sites/default/files/HLTF_Final%20Report_Volume%20I.pdf

[125] United Nations (2013) Report of the Secretary-General on the Situation in the Sahel Region. Available from www.un.org/en/ga/search/view_doc.asp?symbol=S/2013/354

[126] United Nations Development Programme (2013). Group of "Political Champions" pledges support to make Haiti disaster resilient. Available from: www.undp.org/content/undp/en/home/presscenter/pressreleases/2013/04/22/group-of-political-champions-pledges-support-to-make-haiti-disaster-resilient/

[127] See www.un.org/documents/ga/res/46/a46r182.htm

[128] DARA (2010). Inter-Agency Real Time Evaluation of the Humanitarian Response to Pakistan's 2010 Flood Crisis. Available from http://daraint.org/wp-content/uploads/2011/03/Final-Report-RTE-Pakistan-2011.pdf

[129] Stoddard, A., Harmer, A., Haver, K., Salomons, D. & Wheeler, V. (2007). Cluster Approach Evaluation Final Available from: www.humanitarianoutcomes.org/sites/default/files/pdf/ClusterApproachEvaluation.pdf

[130] Slim, H. (2012). IASC Real-Time Evaluation of the Humanitarian Response to the Horn of Africa Drought Crisis in Somalia, Ethiopia and Kenya. Available from: reliefweb.int/sites/reliefweb.int/files/resources/RTE_HoA_SynthesisReport_FINAL.pdf

[131] Evaluation of OCHA's role in Preparedness

[132] Stobbaerts, E., Martin, S. and Derderian, K. (2007). Integration and UN humanitarian reforms. Forced Migration Review N°29. Available from:

[133] Reindorp, N. & Wiles, P. (2001). Humanitarian Coordination: Lessons from Recent Field Experience. Overseas Development Institute. Available from: www.odi.org.uk/sites/odi.org.uk/files/odi-assets/publications-opinion-files/4186.pdf

[134] Bailey, R. (2013). Managing Famine Risk: Linking Early Warning to Early Action. Chatham House. April. Available from: www.chathamhouse.org/sites/default/files/public/Research/Energy,%20Environment%20and%20Development/0413r_earlywarnings.pdf

[135] Bailey, R. (2013). Managing Famine Risk: Linking Early Warning to Early Action. Chatham House. Available from: www.chathamhouse.org/sites/default/files/public/Research/Energy,%20Environment%20and%20Development/0413r_earlywarnings.pdf

[136] Independent Research Forum (2015). Post-2015: framing a new approach to sustainable development. Available from: sustainabledevelopment.un.org/content/documents/1690IRF%20Framework%20Paper.pdf

[137] World Bank (2013) World Development Report 2014: Risk and Opportunity. Available from: econ.worldbank.org/WBSITE/EXTERNAL/EXTDEC/EXTRESEARCH/EXTWDRS/EXTNWDR2013/0,,contentMDK:23330018~pagePK:8258258~piPK:8258412~theSitePK:8258025,00.html

[138] Global Facility for Disaster Risk Reduction Available (2008). Mozambique: Disaster Risk Management Programs for Priority Countries from: gfdrr.org/ctrydrmnotes/Mozambique.pdf

[139] Global Facility for Disaster Risk Reduction Available (2008). Mozambique: Disaster Risk Management Programs for Priority Countries from: gfdrr.org/ctrydrmnotes/Mozambique.pdf

[140] Available from: www.wmo.int/pages/prog/dra/documents/CDSCaseStudy_Mozambique_V2_Withpictures.pdf

[141] Friends of Niger (2012). Nigeriens Feed Nigeriens The 3N Initiative Nigériens Nourissent Nigériens. The Camel Express. September. Volume 27: Issue 2. Available from: http://www.friendsofniger.org/pdf/CEX_Sep_2012.pdf

[142] United Kingdom (2013). National Risk Register of Civil Emergencies. Available from: www.gov.uk/government/uploads/system/uploads/attachment_data/file/211867/NationalRiskRegister2013_amended.pdf

[143] Food and Agriculture Organization of the United Nations (2013). Situation Update. The Sahel Crisis. Available from: www.fao.org/fileadmin/user_upload/emergencies/docs/SITUATION%20UPDATE%20Sahel%2017%2006%202013.pdf

[144] United Nations World Food Programme (2013). The Economics of Early Response and Resilience in Niger. Available from: www.gov.uk/government/uploads/system/uploads/attachment_data/file/228502/TEERR_Niger_Background_Report.pdf

[145] United Kingdom (2013). National Risk Register of Civil Emergencies. Available from: www.gov.uk/government/uploads/system/uploads/attachment_data/file/211867/NationalRiskRegister2013_amended.pdf

[146] The Netherlands Working with scenarios, risk assessment and capabilities in the National Safety and Security Strategy of the Netherlands. Available from: www.preventionweb.net/files/26422_guidancemethodologynationalsafetyan.pdf

[147] World Bank (2013) World Development Report 2014: Risk and Opportunity. Available from: siteresources.worldbank.org/EXTNWDR2013/Resources/8258024-1352909193861/8936935-1356011448215/8986901-1380046989056/WDR-2014_Complete_Report.pdf

[148] Anderson, M. B., Brown, D, & Jean, I. (2012). Time to Listen: Hearing people on the Receiving End of International Aid. Available from: www.cdacollaborative.org/media/60478/Time-to-Listen-Book.pdf

[149] IASC (2012). Proposal for an IASC, UNDG, UNISDR Common Framework for Capacity Development for Preparedness, and for it implementation. 83rd Working Group Meeting on Preparedness. 14-15 November.

[150] Bailey, R. (2013). Managing Famine Risk: Linking Early Warning to Early Action. Chatham House. April. Available from: www.chathamhouse.org/sites/default/files/public/Research/Energy,%20Environment%20and%20Development/0413r_earlywarnings.pdf

[151] Hillier, D. & Castillo, G.E. (2013). No Accident: Resilience and the inequality of risk.

[152] Bailey, R. (2013). Managing Famine Risk: Linking Early Warning to Early Action. Chatham House. April. Available from: www.chathamhouse.org/sites/default/files/public/Research/Energy,%20Environment%20and%20Development/0413r_earlywarnings.pdf

[153] United Nations Office for the Coordination of Humanitarian Affairs (2013) Humanitarianism in the Network Age. Available from: docs.unocha.org/sites/dms/Documents/WEB%20Humanitarianism%20in%20the%20Network%20Age%20vF%20single.pdf

[154] Partners for Resilience (2013). Putting Resilience into Practice. Available from: www.climatecentre.org/downloads/File/PFR/NLRC_PfR_vision%206p%20web.pdf

[155] Red Cross/Red Crescent Climate Centre, 2013: Minimum Standards for local climate – smart disaster risk reduction. Available from: www.climatecentre.org/downloads/File/Minimum%20Standards/Minimum%20Standards%20for%20climate-smart%20DRR%20%202.0%20NOV%202013.pdf

[156] Aguaconsult Ltd. (2008). Evaluation of Disaster Risk Reduction Mainstreaming in DG ECHO's Humanitarian Action : Final Report. Available from: www.preventionweb.net/files/8726_DRRMainstreaming1.pdf

[157] United Nations Office for the Coordination of Humanitarian Affairs (2013). Disaster Response in Asia and the Pacific: A Guide to International Tools and Services. Available from: reliefweb.int/sites/reliefweb.int/files/resources/Disaster%20Response%20in%20Asia%20Pacific_A%20Guide%20to%20Intl%20Tools%20Services.pdf

[158] United Nations International Strategy for Disaster Reduction (2013). Disaster Risk Reduction in the United Nations: Roles, Mandates and Results of key UN entities. Available from: www.unisdr.org/files/32918_drrintheun2013.pdf

[159] United Nations (2005). Hyogo Framework for Action 2005-2015. Available from: www.unisdr.org/files/1037_hyogoframeworkforactionenglish.pdf

[160] United Nations (2013). United Nations Plan of Action on Disaster Risk Reduction for Resilience. Available at: www.preventionweb.net/files/33703_actionplanweb14.06cs[1].pdf

[161] European Union (2013). Sahel – AGIR. Available from: ec.europa.eu/echo/policies/resilience/agir_en.htm

[162] European Union. (2013) AGIR- One year on. Available from: europa.eu/rapid/press-release_SPEECH-13-987_en.htm

[163] See www.cadri.net/

[164] United Nations Development Programme (UNDP). (2012). Evaluation of the Capacity for Disaster Reduction Initiative (CADRI) Available from: http://erc.undp.org/evaluationadmin/manageevaluation/viewevaluationdetail.html?evalid=6161

[165] United Nations Development Programme (UNDP). (2012). Evaluation of the Capacity for Disaster Reduction Initiative (CADRI) Available from: http://erc.undp.org/evaluationadmin/manageevaluation/viewevaluationdetail.html?evalid=6161

[166] United Nations Conference on Environment & Development (1992). Agenda 21 Available from: sustainabledevelopment.un.org/content/documents/Agenda21.pdf

[167] United Nations General Assembly (2000) 55/2. United Nations Millenium Declaration. Available from www.un.org/millennium/declaration/ares552e.htm

[168] World Bank & Global Facility for Disaster Reduction and Recovery (2013). Building Resilience: Integrating Climate and Disaster Risk into Development. Available from: www-wds.worldbank.org/external/default/WDSContentServer/WDSP/IB/2013/11/14/000456286_20131114153130/Rendered/PDF/826480WP0v10Bu0130Box37986200OUO090.pdf

[169] United Nations Development Programme, UNICEF, Oxfam & World Bank (2013). Disaster risk reduction makes development sustainable. Available from: http://www.undp.org/content/dam/undp/library/crisis%20prevention/UNDP_CPR_CTA_20140901.pdf

[170] United Nations (2005). Hyogo Framework for Action 2005-2015. Available from: www.unisdr.org/files/1037_hyogoframeworkforactionenglish.pdf

[171] Shepherd, A., Mitchell, T., Lewis, K., Lenhardt, A., Jones, L., Scott, L., Muir-Wood, R. (2013) The geography of poverty, disasters and climate extremes in 2030. ODI. Available from: www.odi.org.uk/sites/odi.org.uk/files/odi-assets/publications-opinion-files/8633.pdf

[172] Shepherd, A., Mitchell, T., Lewis, K., Lenhardt, A., Jones, L., Scott, L., Muir-Wood, R. (2013) The geography of poverty, disasters and climate extremes in 2030. ODI. Available from: www.odi.org.uk/sites/odi.org.uk/files/odi-assets/publications-opinion-files/8633.pdf

[173] World Bank & Global Facility for Disaster Reduction and Recovery (2013). Building Resilience: Integrating Climate and Disaster Risk into Development. Available from: www-wds.worldbank.org/external/default/WDSContentServer/WDSP/IB/2013/11/14/000456286_20131114153130/Rendered/PDF/826480WP0v10Bu0130Box37986200OUO090.pdf

[174] United Nations Office for the Coordination of Humanitarian Affairs (2013). Unpublished research.

[175] United Nations Office for the Coordination of Humanitarian Affairs (2013). Position Paper and Key Messages: Humanitarian Concerns in the post-2015 Development Agenda. Available from: docs.unocha.org/sites/dms/Documents/Position%20Paper_Humanitarian%20role%20in%20post-2015%20development_FINAL.pdf

[176] Mitchell, T., Jones, L., Lovell, E., Comba, E. (2013) (eds) Disaster risk management in post-2015 development goals: potential targets and indicators. London: Overseas Development Institute. Available from: www.odi.org.uk/sites/odi.org.uk/files/odi-assets/publications-opinion-files/8354.pdf

[177] Available from www.ifrc.org/Global/Publications/disasters/vca/whats-vca-en.pdf

[178] REACH (2013). What is REACH? Available from: www.reach-initiative.org/reach-overview/reachoverview

[179] REACH (2013). What is REACH? Available from: www.reach-initiative.org/reach-overview/reachoverview

[180] IFRC. Disaster Preparedness Tools. Available from: www.ifrc.org/en/what-we-do/disaster-management/preparing-for-disaster/disaster-preparedness-tools/disaster-preparedness-tools/

[181] Index for Risk Management. An Open Humanitarian Risk Index. Available from: inform.jrc.ec.europa.eu/

[182] Change Assembly (2012). Hunchworks. Available from: www.changeassembly.com/hunchworks/

[183] United Nations Office for the Coordination of Humanitarian Affairs (2013). Unpublished research.

[184] World Meteorological Organization (2010). Regional Climate Outlook Forums. Available from: www.wmo.int/pages/prog/wcp/wcasp/documents/RCOFsBrochure.pdf

[185] Change Assembly (2012). Hunchworks. Available from: www.changeassembly.com/hunchworks/

[186] De Groeve, T., Vernaccini, L., and Pljansek, K. (2013). Index for Risk Management - InfoRM: Concept and Methodology. European Commission JRC Scientific and Policy Reports.

[187] United Nations Office for the Coordination of Humanitarian Affairs (2013). Humanitarian Needs Overview 2014. Available from: assessments.humanitarianresponse.info/files/HNO_Guidance_and_Template_2014.pdf

[188] International Federation of Red Cross and Red Crescent Societies (2013). Preparedness saved thousands of lives during Cyclone Phailin; now the recovery begins. Available at: www.ifrc.org/en/news-and-media/news-stories/asia-pacific/india/recovering-from-cyclone-phailin-survivors-face-massive-hardships--63582/

[189] United Nations International Strategy for Disaster Reduction (2006). Global Survey of Early Warning Systems: An assessment of capacities, gaps and opportunities towards building a comprehensive global early warning system for all natural hazards. Available from: www.unisdr.org/files/3612_GlobalSurveyofEarlyWarningSystems.pdf

[190] World Bank (2013) World Development Report 2014: Risk and Opportunity. Available from: siteresources.worldbank.org/EXTNWDR2013/Resources/8258024-1352909193861/8936935-1356011448215/8986901-1380046989056/WDR-2014_Complete_Report.pdf

[191] United Nations (2006) Global Survey of Early Warning Systems. Available from: www.unisdr.org/files/3612_GlobalSurveyofEarlyWarningSystems.pdf

[192] United Nations (2011) Preventive Diplomacy: Delivering Results. Available from: www.un.org/wcm/webdav/site/undpa/shared/undpa/pdf/SG%20Report%20on%20Preventive%20Diplomacy.pdf

[193] UN Security Council (2011) Security Council Pledges Strenghtened UN Effectiveness in Preventing Conflict, including through use of early warning, preventive deployment, mediation. www.un.org/News/Press/docs/2011/sc10392.doc.htm

[194] Perry, C. (2013). Machine Learning and Conflict Prediction: A Use Case. Stability: International Journal of Security and Development 2(3):56. Available from: dx.doi.org/10.5334/sta.cr

[195] Checchi, F. & Courtland Robinson, W. (2013). Mortality among populations of southern and central Somalia affected by severe food insecurity and famine during 2010-2012. A Study commissioned by FAO/FSNAU and FEWS NET. London School of Hygiene and Tropical Medicine and Johns Hopkins University Bloomberg School of Public Health

[196] Slim, H. (2012). IASC Real-Time Evaluation of the Humanitarian Response to the Horn of Africa Drought Crisis in Somalia, Ethiopia and Kenya. Available from: reliefweb.int/sites/reliefweb.int/files/resources/RTE_HoA_SynthesisReport_FINAL.pdf

[197] DFID (2012). Progress Update DFID Management Response to the Independent Commission for Aid Impact recommendations on: DFID's Humanitarian Emergency Response in the Horn of Africa. Available from: www.gov.uk/government/uploads/system/uploads/attachment_data/file/180825/March_2013_ICAI_Progress_Update_-_DFIDs_Emergency_Response_in_the_Horn_of_Africa_P1.pdf

[198] Food Security and Nutrition Working Group (2013) Update. Available from: www.disasterriskreduction.net/fileadmin/user_upload/drought/docs/FSNWG%20Update%20October%2020131114.pdf

[199] Slim, H. (2012). IASC Real-Time Evaluation of the Humanitarian Response to the Horn of Africa Drought Crisis in Somalia, Ethiopia and Kenya. Available from: reliefweb.int/sites/reliefweb.int/files/resources/RTE_HoA_SynthesisReport_FINAL.pdf

[200] World Bank & Global Facility for Disaster Reduction and Recovery (2012). The Sendai Report. Managing Disaster Risk for a Resilient Future. Available from: www.gfdrr.org/sites/gfdrr.org/files/Sendai_Report_051012.pdf

[201] United Nations Development Group (2010). How to Prepare an UNDAF. Available from: www.undg.org/docs/11096/How-to-Prepare-an-UNDAF-(Part-I).pdf

[202] United Nations Office for the Coordination of Humanitarian Affairs (2013). Strategic Response Plan Guidance. Available from: docs.unocha.org/sites/dms/CAP/2014_SRP_guidance-27_Sep_2013_EN.pdf

[203] Anderson, M. B., Brown, D, & Jean, I. (2012). Time to Listen: Hearing people on the Receiving End of International Aid. Available from: www.cdacollaborative.org/media/60478/Time-to-Listen-Book.pdf

[204] USAID (2012). Building Resilience to Recurrent Crisis: USAID Policy and Program Guidance. Available from: transition.usaid.gov/resilience/USAIDResiliencePolicyGuidanceDocument.pdf

[205] FAO, UNICEF, WFP (2012). A Strategy for Enhancing Resilience in Somalia. July. Available from: www.fao.org/fileadmin/templates/cfs_high_level_forum/documents/Brief-Resilience-_JointStrat_-_Final_Draft.pdf.

[206] United Nations Office for the Coordination of Humanitarian Affairs (2013). Exchange of Practices and Lessons Learnt on Resilience Building in the Horn of Africa and the Sahel Regions. Workshop Report. Available from: www.urd.org/IMG/pdf/Horn_Sahel_Resilience_Workshop_Report_-_final.pdf

[207] Sahel Working Group (2011). Escaping the hunger cycle: pathways to resilience in the Sahel. Available from: www.e-alliance.ch/fileadmin/user_upload/docs/Publications/Food/2012/Escaping_the_Hunger_Cycle_English.pdf

[208] United Nations Office for the Coordination of Humanitarian Affairs (2013). Humanitarian actors in the Sahel start work on a three-year response plan. Press Release. Available from: reliefweb.int/sites/reliefweb.int/files/resources/2013.28.11%20-%20Press%20release%20HNO.pdf

[209] United Nations Office for the Coordination of Humanitarian Affairs (2012). Somalia Consolidated Appeal 2013-2015. Available from: docs.unocha.org/sites/dms/CAP/CAP_2013_Somalia.pdf

[210] United Nations Office for the Coordination of Humanitarian Affairs (2012). Reference Guide for Developing the 2013 Consolidated Appeals.
Available from: docs.unocha.org/sites/dms/CAP/CAP_2013_Reference_Guide.pdf

[211] United Nations Office for the Coordination of Humanitarian Affairs (2010). Consolidated Appeal for Kenya 2011+ Emergency Response Humanitarian Plan. Available from: docs.unocha.org/sites/dms/CAP/2011_Kenya_EHRP.pdf

[212] DARA (2011). The Humanitarian Response Index 2011. Addressing the Gender Challenge. Available from: daraint.org/wp-content/uploads/2012/03/HRI_2011_Complete_Report.pdf

[213] United Nations Office for the Coordination of Humanitarian Affairs (2013). Exchange of Practices and Lessons Learnt on Resilience Building in the Horn of Africa and the Sahel Regions. Workshop Report. Available from: www.urd.org/IMG/pdf/Horn_Sahel_Resilience_Workshop_Report_-_final.pdf

[214] OXFAM (2012). Building Resilience in Eastern Indonesia – Effectiveness Review. Full Technical Report. Available from: reliefweb.int/sites/reliefweb.int/files/resources/er-building-resilience-indonesia-effectiveness-review-081012-full-report-en.pdf

[215] The Jakarta Post (2013). Communities can protect themselves from natural disasters, says Oxfam.
Available from: www.thejakartapost.com/news/2013/03/24/communities-can-protect-themselves-natural-disasters-says-oxfam.html

[216] Harvey, P. & Bailey, S. (2011). Good Practice Review. Cash transfer programming in emergencies. Humanitarian Practice Network. Overseas Development Institute. Available from: www.odihpn.org/hpn-resources/good-practice-reviews/cash-transfer-programming-in-emergencies

[217] Woodke, J. (2012). Humanitarian Exchange Magazine. Cash transfers and vulnerability in Niger. Humanitarian Practice Network. Overseas Development Institute. Available from: www.odihpn.org/humanitarian-exchange-magazine/issue-55/cash-transfers-and-vulnerability-in-niger

[218] United Nations World Food Programme (2013). Report of the External Auditor on Use of Cash and Vouchers. Available from: documents.wfp.org/stellent/groups/public/documents/eb/wfpdoc062619.pdf

[219] United Nations World Food Programme (2013). Report of the External Auditor on Use of Cash and Vouchers. Available from: documents.wfp.org/stellent/groups/public/documents/eb/wfpdoc062619.pdf

[220] The Cash Learning Partnership (2013). Is Emergency Cash Transfer Programming (CTP) 'fit for the future'?. Available from: http://www.cashlearning.org/downloads/uptake-by-governments-final2-updated-13-01-2014.pdf

[221] Pasteur, K. (2011). From Vulnerability to Resilience A framework for analysis and action to build community resilience. Practical Action Publishing. Available from: cdn1.practicalaction.org/v/u/4dc2a064-3484-4c1b-aec1-75230aeb3a10.pdf

[222] IRIN (2011). KENYA: Demo Hassan, "For 40 years, food aid has been routine"
Available from: www.irinnews.org/hov/93592/kenya-demo-hassan-for-40-years-food-aid-has-been-routine

[223] Kellett, J. & Peters, K. (2014). Dare to prepare: taking risk seriously. Financing emergency preparedness: from fighting crisis to managing risk. Overseas Development Institute. Available from: www.odi.org.uk/sites/odi.org.uk/files/odi-assets/publications-opinion-files/8748.pdf

[224] Sparks, D. (2012). Aid investments in disaster risk reduction - rhetoric to action. Available from: http://www.globalhumanitarianassistance.org/wp-content/uploads/2012/10/Aid-investments-in-disaster-risk-reduction-rhetoric-to-action-Dan-Sparks1.pdf

[225] Overseas Development Institute & Global Facility for Disaster Reduction and Recovery (2013). International Financing for Disaster Risk Management: The 20-Year Story (1991-2010).
Available from: www.odi.org.uk/sites/odi.org.uk/files/odi-assets/publications-opinion-files/8398.pdf

[226] Kellett, J. & Caravani, A. (2013). Financing Disaster Risk Reduction. A 20 year story of international aid. Overseas Development Institute & Global Facility for Disaster Reduction and Recovery. Available from: www.odi.org.uk/sites/odi.org.uk/files/odi-assets/publications-opinion-files/8574.pdf

[227] Kellett J. & Sparks, D. (2012). Disaster risk reduction: Spending where it should count. Available from: http://www.globalhumanitarianassistance.org/wp-content/uploads/2012/03/GHA-Disaster-Risk-Report.pdf

[228] Global Humanitarian Assistance (2013). Global Humanitarian Assistance Report 2013. Available from: www.globalhumanitarianassistance.org/wp-content/uploads/2013/07/GHA-Report-20131.pdf

[229] Kellett, J. & Peters, K. (2014). Dare to prepare: taking risk seriously. Financing emergency preparedness: from fighting crisis to managing risk. Overseas Development Institute. Available from: www.odi.org.uk/sites/odi.org.uk/files/odi-assets/publications-opinion-files/8748.pdf

[230] Sparks, D. (2012). Aid investments in disaster risk reduction - rhetoric to action. Global Humanitarian Assistance. Available from: www.globalhumanitarianassistance.org/wp-content/uploads/2012/10/Aid-investments-in-disaster-risk-reduction-rhetoric-to-action-Dan-Sparks1.pdf

[231] Global Humanitarian Assistance (2013). Global Humanitarian Assistance Report 2013. Available from: www.globalhumanitarianassistance.org/wp-content/uploads/2013/07/GHA-Report-20131.pdf
[232] Bailey, R. (2013). pers. comm.

[233] Kellett, J. & Peters, K. (2014). Dare to prepare: taking risk seriously. Summary. Financing emergency preparedness: from fighting crisis to managing risk. Overseas Development Institute. Available from: http://www.odi.org.uk/files/odi-assets/publications-opinion-files/8747.pdf

234 Kellett J. & Sparks, D. (2012). Disaster risk reduction: Spending where it should count. Available from: http://www.globalhumanitarianassistance.org/wp-content/uploads/2012/03/GHA-Disaster-Risk-Report.pdf

235 Index for Risk Management. An Open Humanitarian Risk Index. Available from: inform.jrc.ec.europa.eu/

236 OECD (2013). Ensuring Fragile States Are Not Left Behind. 2013 Factsheet on resource flows and trends. Available from: www.oecd.org/dac/incaf/factsheet%202013%20resource%20flows%20final.pdf

237 Kellett, J. & Caravani, A. (2013). Financing Disaster Risk Reduction. A 20 year story of international aid. Overseas Development Institute & Global Facility for Disaster Reduction and Recovery. Available from: www.odi.org.uk/sites/odi.org.uk/files/odi-assets/publications-opinion-files/8574.pdf

238 The United Nations Office for Disaster Risk Reduction (2013). Donors back DRR investment tracking. Available from: www.unisdr.org/archive/34772

239 USAID (2012). Remarks by Dennis Weller, Mission Director Ethiopia on Launch of the Pastoralist Areas Resiliency Improvement through Market Expansion (PRIME) Project. Available from: www.usaid.gov/sites/default/files/documents/1860/MD%20Remarks%20PRIME%20Launch%20%2012-18-12.pdf

240 Anderson, M., Brown, D. & Jean, I. (2012). Time to Listen, Hearing People on the Receiving End of International Aid. CDA Collaborative Learning Projects. Available from: www.cdacollaborative.org/media/60478/Time-to-Listen-Book.pdf

241 Good Humanitarian Donorship. Principles and Good Practice of Humanitarian Donorship. Available from: www.goodhumanitariandonorship.org/Libraries/Ireland_Doc_Manager/EN-23-Principles-and-Good-Practice-of-Humanitarian-Donorship.sflb.ashx

242 Bailey, R. (2013). Managing Famine Risk: Linking Early Warning to Early Action. Chatham House. Available from: www.chathamhouse.org/sites/default/files/public/Research/Energy,%20Environment%20and%20Development/0413r_earlywarnings.pdf

243 Index for Risk Management. An Open Humanitarian Risk Index. Available from: http://inform.jrc.ec.europa.eu/

244 United Nations Office for the Coordination of Humanitarian Affairs (2013). Global Overview of 2012 Pooled Funding: CERF, CHFs and ERFs. Available from: docs.unocha.org/sites/dms/Documents/Global%20Overview%20of%202012%20Pooled%20Funding%20-%20CERF,%20CHFs%20and%20ERFs.pdf

245 Kellett, J. & Peters, K. (2014). Dare to prepare: taking risk seriously. Financing emergency preparedness: from fighting crisis to managing risk. Overseas Development Institute. Available from: www.odi.org.uk/sites/odi.org.uk/files/odi-assets/publications-opinion-files/8748.pdf

246 FEWSNET (2011). Executive Brief, Niger. Available from www.fews.net/docs/Publications/Niger_EB_2011_10_en_ext.pdf

247 United Nations Office for the Coordination of Humanitarian Affairs (2013). Supporting Early Action Through the Central Emergency Response Fund (CERF) and Country-Based Pooled Funds (CBPFs). Available from: docs.unocha.org/sites/dms/CERF/Pooled%20Funds%20and%20Early%20Action%20CERF.pdf

248 ReliefWeb (2013). South Sudan: $56.5 million for aid and emergency preparedness. Available from: reliefweb.int/report/south-sudan-republic/south-sudan-565-million-aid-and-emergency-preparedness

249 IRIN (2013). Bridging the gap between relief and development in DRC. Available from: www.irinnews.org/report/98288/bridging-the-gap-between-relief-and-development-in-drc

250 Goyder, H. (2011). Evaluation of the Common Humanitarian Fund. Synthesis Report. Channel Research. Available from: ochanet.unocha.org/p/Documents/CHF_Evaluation_Synthesis_Report.pdf

251 Harding, J. (2013). pers. comm.

[252] IRIN (2013). Bridging the gap between relief and development in DRC. Available from: www.irinnews.org/report/98288/bridging-the-gap-between-relief-and-development-in-drc

[253] IPCC (2012). Managing the Risks of Extreme Events and Disasters to Advance Climate Change Adaptation. Special Report of the Intergovernmental Panel on Climate Change. Available from: ipcc-wg2.gov/SREX/images/uploads/SREX-All_FINAL.pdf

[254] Caribbean Catastrophe Risk Insurance Facility (2010). Caribbean Catastrophe Risk Insurance Facility. Available from: www.ccrif.org/sites/default/files/publications/CCRIFBrochure20101129.pdf

[255] Caribbean Catastrophe Risk Insurance Facility (2012). Semiannual Report June-November 2012. Available from: www.ccrif.org/sites/default/files/publications/CCRIF_Semiannual_Report_June_November_2012.pdf

[256] Caribbean Catastrophe Risk Insurance Facility (2010). CCRIF News Volume 2, Number 1. Available from: www.ccrif.org/sites/default/files/publications/CCRIF_News_September_2010.pdf

[257] African Risk Capacity (2013). African Risk Capacity. Available from: www.africanriskcapacity.org

[258] International Food Policy Research Institute (2013). Cost-Benefit Analysis of the African Risk Capacity Facility. Available from: www.ifpri.org/publication/cost-benefit-analysis-african-risk-capacity-facility

[259] African Risk Capacity. (2013). The Cost of Drought in Africa. Available from www.africanriskcapacity.org.

[260] Caribbean Catastrophe Risk Insurance Facility (2010). CCRIF Pays Government of Anguilla US$4.28 Million following passage of Hurricane Earl. Available from: www.ccrif.org/sites/default/files/publications/CCRIF_News_September_2010.pdf

[261] Hui, J. (2013). The Rise of Microinsurance. Available from: www.rmmagazine.com/2013/03/08/the-rise-of-microinsurance

[262] Lloyd's (2010). Insurance in developing countries: Exploring opportunities in microinsurance. Available from: www.lloyds.com/~/media/Lloyds/Reports/360/360%20Other/InsuranceInDevelopingCountries.pdf

[263] Swiss Re (2010). Sigma No. 6: Microinsurance: risk protection for 4 billion people. Available from : media.swissre.com/documents/sigma6_2010_en.pdf

[264] Oxfam (2010). HARITA Quarterly Report October-December 2010. Available from: www.oxfamamerica.org/files/harita-quarterly-report-oct-dec-2010-screen.pdf

[265] International Research Institute for Climate and Society, Columbia University (2012). Poor Ethiopian Farmers Receive "Unprecedented" Insurance Payout. Available from: iri.columbia.edu/news/poor-ethiopian-farmers-receive-unprecedented-insurance-payout/

[266] Oxfam (2010). HARITA Quarterly Report October-December 2010. Available from: www.oxfamamerica.org/files/harita-quarterly-report-oct-dec-2010-screen.pdf

[267] Oxfam. Medhin Reda Looks to Weather Insurance to Solve Problems. Available from: www.oxfamamerica.org/articles/medhin-reda-looks-to-weather-insurance-to-solve-problems

[268] World Bank (2013). World Development Report 2014: Risk and Opportunity, Managing Risk in Development. Available from: siteresources.worldbank.org/EXTNWDR2013/Resources/8258024-1352909193861/8936935-1356011448215/8986901-1380046989056/WDR-2014_Complete_Report.pdf

[269] Mobarak, A. M. & Rosenzweig, M. R. (2012). Selling Formal Insurance to the Informally Insured. Available at: papers.ssrn.com/sol3/papers.cfm?abstract_id=2009528

[270] Dubois, P., Jullieny, B. & Magnacz, T. (2007). Formal and Informal Risk Sharing in LDCs: Theory and Empirical Evidence. Available from: idei.fr/doc/by/dubois/formal_informal.pdf

[271] Inter-agency Standing Committee (2010). RC Terms of Reference. Available from: www.humanitarianinfo.org/iasc/pageloader.aspx?page=content-subsidi-common-default&sb=77

[272] Inter-agency Standing Committee (2010). Handbook for RCs and HCs on Emergency Preparedness and Response. Available from: www.humanitarianinfo.org/iasc/pageloader.aspx?page=content-subsidi-common-default&sb=77

[273] Inter-agency Standing Committee (2012). Proposal for an IASC, UNDG, UNISDR Common Framework for Capacity Development for Preparedness, and for its implementation.

[274] Hui, J. (2013). The Rise of Microinsurance. Risk Management. Available from: www.rmmagazine.com/2013/03/08/the-rise-of-microinsurance/

[275] Stoddard, A. & Harmer, A. (2005). Room to Manoeuvre: Challenges of Linking Humanitarian Action and Post- Conflict Recovery in the New Global Security Environment. Available from: hdr.undp.org/en/content/room-manoeuvre

[276] Slim, H. & Bradley, M. (2013) Principled Humanitarian Action & Ethical Tensions in Multi-Mandate Organizations in Armed Conflict, World Vision. Available from: www.humanitarianinfo.org/iasc/downloaddoc.aspx?docID=6519

[277] Hillier, D. (2013). pers. comm.

[278] United Nations Office for the Coordination of Humanitarian Affairs (2013). Interview: "Business as usual doesn't cut it". Available from: www.unocha.org/top-stories/all-stories/interview-%E2%80%9Cbusiness-usual-doesn%E2%80%99t-cut-it%E2%80%9D

[279] IRIN (2012). SAHEL: What went right in the crisis response? Available from: www.irinnews.org/report/96632/sahel-what-went-right-in-the-crisis-response

[280] United Nations Office for the Coordination of Humanitarian Affairs (2013). Interview: Regional Humanitarian Coordinator for the Sahel. Available from: www.unocha.org/top-stories/all-stories/interview-regional-humanitarian-coordinator-sahel

[281] United Nations Development Programme (2013). Political Champions: no development without disaster risk reduction. Available from: www.undp.org/content/undp/en/home/presscenter/pressreleases/2013/09/25/political-champions-no-development-without-disaster-risk-reduction/

[282] Turkcell (2011). Annual Report 2011. Available from: yatirimci-2011-eng.turkcell.com.tr/downloads/Turkcell-AR-2011-ENG.pdf

[283] United Nations Development Programme (2012). Act Now, Save Later: new UN social media campaign launched. Available from: www.undp.org/content/undp/en/home/presscenter/articles/2012/07/02/act-now-save-later-new-un-social-media-campaign-launched-/

[284] World Health Organization (2013). Global Status Report on Road Safety. Available from: www.who.int/iris/bitstream/10665/78256/1/9789241564564_eng.pdf

[285] European Commission (2010). Towards a European road safety area: policy orientations on road safety 2011-2020. Available from: ec.europa.eu/transport/road_safety/pdf/com_20072010_en.pdf

[286] Turkcell (2011). Annual Report 2011. Available from: yatirimci-2011-eng.turkcell.com.tr/downloads/Turkcell-AR-2011-ENG.pdf